Writing Effective Software Documentation

Patricia A. Williams
Pamela S. Beason

SCOTT, FORESMAN AND COMPANY

Glenview, Illinois   London

To my children: Chris, Doug, Nancy, and Steve.

—P.W.

To my father, who taught me to dream and to laugh.

—P.B.

Library of Congress Cataloging-in-Publication Data

Williams, Patricia A.
    Writing effective software documentation / Patricia A. Williams,
Pamela S. Beason.
        p.   cm.
    Includes bibliographical references.
    ISBN 0-673-46163-7
    1. Electronic data processing documentation.   2. Computer software—
Development.   I. Beason, Pamela S.   II. Title.
QA76.9.D6W55   1990
005.1'5—dc20   89-29973
                                                                    CIP

1 2 3 4 5 6 MVN 94 93 92 91 90 89

ISBN 0-673-46163-7

Scott, Foresman professional books are available for bulk sales at quantity discounts.
For information, please contact Marketing Manager, Professional Books Group,
Scott, Foresman and Company, 1900 East Lake Avenue, Glenview, IL 60025.

TRADEMARKS

Aldus FreeHand is a trademark, and Aldus, Persuasion, and PageMaker are registered trademarks of the Aldus Corporation.

Amí is a registered trademark of the SAMNA Corporation.

Apple is a registered trademark, and Macintosh, Macintosh II, and HyperCard are trademarks of Apple Computer, Inc.

AST is a registered trademark of AST Research, Inc.

Lotus and 1-2-3 are registered trademarks of Lotus Development Corporation.

MacLinkPlus is a trademark of the DataViz Corp.

Microrim and R:BASE are registered trademarks of Microrim, Inc.

Microsoft, MS-DOS, and QuickC are registered trademarks of the Microsoft Corporation.

PFS and First Choice are registered trademarks of Software Publishing Corporation.

RAPID RELAY is a trademark of Systems Management Associates, Inc.

SnapShot is a trademark of BioScan Inc.

Ventura Publisher is a registered trademark of Ventura Software, Inc.

who•what•when is a trademark of Chronos Software, Inc.

Wizard PC-Link is a trademark and Traveling Software and the Traveling suitcase logo are registered trademarks of Traveling Software, Inc.

Xerox is a trademark of the Xerox Corporation.

ACKNOWLEDGMENTS

The authors wish to thank the following software publishers for their generosity in supplying the many excerpts used in this book.

Excerpts from *Learning Aldus FreeHand, Aldus SnapShot Installation Guide, Aldus SnapShot User Manual* used with the express permission of the Aldus Corporation. © Aldus Corporation 1988.

Excerpts from the *Amí User's Guide* and *Amí Quick Reference Card* used with permission of the SAMNA Corporation.

Excerpts from the *AST Operating System Manual Version 3.3* used with permission of AST Research, Inc.

INTRODUCTION

Effective documentation and successful software go hand in hand. As technical writers with extensive experience, we have seen firsthand how poor documentation—whether due to indifference, inadequate planning, or lack of writing skill—can hamper even the most brilliant and innovative of software programs. When software is competing with other programs in the marketplace, the quality of the documentation can make or break sales. When software is developed for in-house use, the quality of the documentation affects time spent in training employees, efficiency on the job, and, ultimately, the organization's profits.

Effective documentation makes for successful software because it helps users master the software. *Writing* effective documentation is very much like any other project; with proper planning and the application of tried-and-tested techniques, you're sure to succeed. *Writing Effective Software Documentation* is a compilation of those tried-and-tested techniques.

WHO THIS BOOK IS FOR

Writing Effective Software Documentation is for anyone who has to write documentation that explains software applications, systems, and languages to users, including

- O independent programmers who develop software to sell to the general public or on contract for companies
- O programmers who develop software for their companies
- O systems analysts and systems engineers who oversee the development of software for their companies
- O technical writers who document software for companies

No matter what kind of documentation you need to write, this book

○ shows you how to use predeveloped forms during software development to record information that will serve as a basis for your documentation
○ tells you how to plan and manage a documentation project
○ clarifies the types of documentation you should use to reach different kinds of users and achieve different types of goals
○ shows you how to organize each type of documentation
○ gives you concrete writing techniques to make your documents easy to read
○ shows you excerpts from existing documentation to use as models

THE EIGHT MOST IMPORTANT RULES FOR EFFECTIVE DOCUMENTATION

Software documentation has a bad reputation, earned in the early years when developers believed documentation consisted of photocopies of the programmer's notes, stapled together and handed out to users as an afterthought. The prevailing theory was that software, if developed properly, was easy to use, somehow or other *transparent* to the users, and that user documentation was unnecessary. This theory, although trampled by frustrated users and bad reviews in computer magazines, died hard. As a result, documentation has improved greatly. Its bad reputation, however, is proving difficult to overcome.

The mistakes of the past have taught us a lot. The guidelines in *Writing Effective Software Documentation* center around eight very important rules, learned by painful trial and error.

1. Look at the software from the users' point of view.
2. Plan. Before you write, be sure to gather necessary information, analyze, think, and organize.
3. Give users what they need to accomplish the tasks they want to perform.

4. Make everything—structure, language, and page layout—as consistent as possible.

5. Strive for simplicity. Strip away jargon and obscuring theories.

6. Make your writing alive. Use active verbs, and write in the present tense.

7. Use examples and scenarios that are relevant to the users.

8. Lay out manuals and on-line documentation in such a way that users can easily find the information they're looking for. Provide plenty of road signs.

HOW THIS BOOK IS ORGANIZED

Part I Project Planning and Management	Gives an overview of the development process and explains how to create a documentation plan, make a style sheet, and design and illustrate a document.
Part II Organizing Software Documentation	Gives an overview of the different types of documentation and the parts that make up a document. Describes tutorials, procedures guides, reference manuals, quick reference materials, and on-line help systems. Shows examples of each type.
Part III Applying Writing Techniques	Describes writing techniques. Shows how to construct paragraphs; write from the readers' point of view; choose clear and strong language; define, describe, and explain; and write procedures.
Part IV Information Forms	Provides 12 handy forms that you can duplicate and use for compiling information necessary to write user's guides for any software project.

Writing Effective Software Documentation contains the information you need to write effective documentation, documentation that will support the software and ensure its success.

CONTENTS

3

Designing a Document   26

4

Planning the Illustrations   39

5

Setting Standards   56

6

Reviews, Usability Tests, and Revisions   70

7

Corrections, Addenda, and New Versions   84

PART TWO

ORGANIZING SOFTWARE DOCUMENTATION   89

8

Types of Documentation   91

9

The Parts of a Document 96

10

Organizing Tutorials 121

11

Organizing Procedures Guides 144

PART THREE

APPLYING WRITING TECHNIQUES   227

15

Building Paragraphs and Passages   229

16

Writing from the Readers' Viewpoint   242

17

Using Clear and Strong Language   253

PROJECT PLANNING AND MANAGEMENT

The success of any type of documentation project depends on good planning and management practices. In the chaos that often surrounds a software project, people may rush into writing the documentation and give planning short shrift. The lack of planning, however, inevitably results in time wasted later on, when you have to retrace your steps and correct mistakes. We won't even mention the unnecessary frustration and stress you may suffer as a result.

Follow the guidelines described in this part of the book and establish a routine for planning. It will pay off. You'll save yourself a lot of time and frazzled nerves and make everyone happy with the resulting documentation.

CHAPTER 1

The Documentation Development Process

Software development has a rhythm all its own, usually a frantic one. This chapter describes how documentation fits into the process, the steps involved in creating documentation, and how you can develop a realistic schedule.

DOCUMENTATION AS PART OF THE SOFTWARE DEVELOPMENT PROCESS

Generally, every software development project includes nine phases. In a small project, the early phases may be very informal, consisting only of a conversation or two or just some hard thinking and analysis by a lone software developer. In larger projects, on the other hand, each phase

3

may be formally recognized, documented, reviewed, and accepted. The nine phases in a software development project are

1	Feasibility Analysis	The developer (or development team) states the objectives, defines the general requirements, and analyzes the feasibility of undertaking the project.
2	Requirements Definition	The developer defines the program (from the users' perspective) and describes functions, information to be maintained and reported, assumptions, constraints, and impact on the users.
3	Alternatives Analysis	The developer identifies and analyzes two or three alternatives and recommends one of these alternatives for further development.
4	Functional Specifications	The developer defines the operating environment, establishes constraints and assumptions that will govern design, defines data (inputs, files, and outputs), breaks the program into modules, specifies design requirements for data control, and defines processing logic and user interface for functions.

5	Preliminary Design	The developer defines the processes within each module to meet the functional specifications.
6	Detailed Design and Construction	The developer creates a detailed design from the preliminary design modules, followed by code construction and developmental testing.
7	Verification	The developer carries out alpha and beta testing and corrects and streamlines the program.
8	Implementation	The developer formally releases or installs the program. Training of users, if applicable, begins.
9	Maintenance	The developer makes corrections and improvements to the program.

In a small project, the documentation may consist of a programmer's notebook, which documents the software's development, and user documentation.

In a larger project, the documentation may consist of a large document (or set of documents) for each phase and user documentation, which could include user's manuals, reference materials, quick reference guides, and on-line materials.

Figure 1.1 shows how user documentation fits into the overall process.

Phase	User documentation
1 Feasibility Analysis	
2 Requirements Definition	
3 Alternatives Analysis	
4 Functional Specifications	
5 Preliminary Design	Documentation plan
6 Detailed Design and Construction	Outline(s) for user documentation
	First draft(s) of users' manual(s)
	First draft of on-line help system
7 Verification (alpha and beta tests)	Reviews of first drafts
	Usability tests of tutorials and procedures guides
	Review, linking, and testing of on-line systems
	Final drafts of users' manual(s)
	First and final drafts of quick reference pieces
8 Implementation	User documentation completed
9 Maintenance	Revisions and addenda

Figure 1.1. User Documentation in the Software Development Process.

User documentation may consist of one component, such as a procedures guide, or many, such as several printed pieces and on-line materials too. The writer's responsibility may vary; sometimes it entails writing the printed materials alone, sometimes it includes writing both printed and on-line materials. Occasionally, the writer is also responsible for coordinating the production of the printed materials. Whether your responsibilities include the coordination of production or not, some knowledge of the entire process can be very helpful. Figure 1.2 shows the basic steps in producing a single printed document.

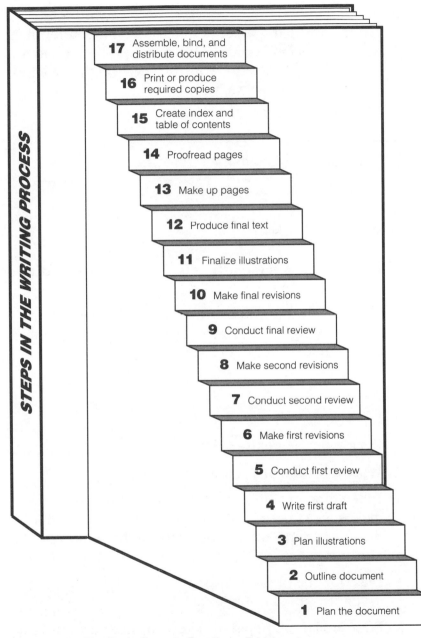

STEPS IN THE WRITING PROCESS

17 Assemble, bind, and distribute documents

16 Print or produce required copies

15 Create index and table of contents

14 Proofread pages

13 Make up pages

12 Produce final text

11 Finalize illustrations

10 Make final revisions

9 Conduct final review

8 Make second revisions

7 Conduct second review

6 Make first revisions

5 Conduct first review

4 Write first draft

3 Plan illustrations

2 Outline document

1 Plan the document

Figure 1.2. The Basic Steps in Creating a Document.

The following sections describe the steps in planning, writing, and producing a user's manual, a quick reference guide, and on-line materials. This description is general; the steps you need to take for your project and the order in which you take them may vary.

STEPS IN THE PLANNING PHASE

DOCUMENTATION PLAN

1. Locate and review existing information, and confer with team members.

2. Decide how many and what types of individual documents (manuals or other printed pieces) and on-line materials are needed.

DOCUMENT PLAN

1. Decide on the goals of the document.

2. Write a profile of the audience.

3. Determine production methods, including the means for creating illustrations, producing a final draft, and reproducing or printing the required number of copies.

4. Describe the physical appearance of the document, its length, size, binding, etc.

5. Put the plan on paper and get it approved.

6. Draft a schedule and get it approved.

7. Create a style guide.

STEPS IN THE OUTLINING AND WRITING PHASE

DOCUMENT OUTLINE

1. Review the information in your documentation plan about the readers and their needs, and the goals of the document.
2. Decide how to organize the document.
3. Draft a preliminary or working outline of the printed documents, including quick reference materials.
4. Draft a preliminary outline of the on-line materials.
5. Review the outlines and revise them if necessary.
6. Get the outlines approved.

FIRST DRAFT

1. Write the first draft.
2. Write or review the first draft of the on-line materials.
3. Make a preliminary list of illustrations.
4. Read and revise the first draft.
5. Update the list of illustrations.
6. Send the draft out for review.

SUBSEQUENT DRAFTS

1. Incorporate comments and corrections from the review.
2. Do any necessary rewriting.
3. Make copies of completed illustrations and insert them in the draft.
4. Proofread and correct the draft, covering both text and illustrations.
5. Send the draft out for review.
6. Review and correct on-line materials.

FINAL DRAFT

1. Incorporate comments and corrections from the review.
2. Read all text and review illustrations, checking for flow, clarity, and completeness.
3. Write quick reference materials.
4. Get final okays on changes from reviewers or supervisor.
5. Have quick reference materials reviewed and proofread.
6. Check text and illustrations for consistency, and proofread for typographical, spelling, or placement errors.
7. Indicate spaces for illustrations. If necessary, mark headings, words or phrases that need special emphasis, and page breaks.
8. Review on-line materials for the final time.
9. Correct quick reference materials.

STEPS IN THE PRODUCTION PHASE

TYPESETTING, PAGE MAKE-UP, AND PRINTING

1. Produce the text by typewriter, word processing software, or computerized typesetting.

2. Proofread the text (or galleys, if the document is commercially typeset).

3. Make up pages, merging text and graphics (either with traditional paste-up methods or with page make-up software).

4. Check for continuity and positioning of illustrations.

5. Number the pages of the document, if necessary.

6. Prepare the table of contents and index.

7. Proofread page numbers for the index and table of contents.

8. If the document is being professionally printed, check the blue line (sample of printed document) for accuracy, consistency, and placement of text on pages.

9. Print or duplicate the required number of copies.

ASSEMBLY, BINDING, AND DISTRIBUTION

1. Collate and assemble the copies.

2. Add bindings or covers.

3. Assemble and wrap the documentation package, if necessary.

4. Distribute.

MAKING A SCHEDULE

Writers are often under a great deal of pressure to deliver a manuscript. Programming and marketing personnel may be unaware of all the steps involved in creating a document or of how much time certain processes—like editing and reviewing—can take. As a result, writers may end up working overtime to meet unrealistic deadlines. This section contains guidelines to help you avoid that stressful situation.

CREATING A PRELIMINARY SCHEDULE

The complexity and length of your schedule depends on the complexity of the program and its documentation. The steps in the scheduling process usually go like this:

1. Pinpoint the delivery dates for the first, second, and final drafts and for the hand-off to the production department.

2. List all of the steps involved in the process.

3. Get estimates on how long it will take to perform each of the necessary steps, consulting with editors, reviewers, proofreaders, artists, word processors, etc.

4. Map out the steps or events on a calendar, counting only work days and making sure major events don't collide with vacations, holidays, or the schedules for other projects.

5. If you can't meet the final deadline with this initial time estimate, go back over the steps to find out where you can save time.

6. Draft the schedule and get commitments from team members.

7. Get the preliminary schedule approved.

8. If necessary, give each team member a copy of the schedule.

UPDATING THE SCHEDULE

Keep in mind that your first schedule will be a rough draft, that changes are inevitable, and that everyone involved must be notified about those changes.

If your project is complex, you may need to appoint a project leader or scheduler to keep track of the document's progress at all stages, to update the schedule each week, and to keep everyone informed of schedule changes.

EXAMPLE OF A SCHEDULE

The following schedule is an example of one created for a moderately long user's manual.

SCHEDULE

Project: ChArtist User's Manual
Project Manager: Joel Geffs
Scheduler: Alice Foster
Weekly meeting: Tuesday 9 a.m., Room 217

Preliminary Schedule

January 13–15	Review document plan and outlines
January 19–20	Revise document plan and outlines
January 25–26	Final review of document plan and outlines
January 27	Begin writing Part I
February 15	Begin planning Part I illustrations
February 29–March 10	Review Part I
March 14–17	Revise Part I
March 21–23	Final review of Part I
	Begin writing Part II and help system
April 7	Begin planning Part II illustrations
April 18–25	Review Part II
	Review help system
April 25–May 6	Revise Part II
	Start production of illustrations
May 9–12	Final review of Part II
May 9	Begin writing appendixes
May 30–June 3	Review appendixes
	Write quick reference guide
	Review illustrations
June 6–10	Revise appendixes
June 6–20	Revise illustrations
June 13–14	Final review of appendixes
	Final review of quick reference guide
	Final review of help system
June 20	Final review of illustrations
June 15–30	Make final corrections
July 4	Hand off to production editor
August 1	Hand off to printer
September 1	Completed documentation delivered by printer

Knowledge of the documentation process makes planning and managing a documentation project and completing it in a timely manner much easier.

CHAPTER 2

Creating a Documentation Plan

Careful planning helps you create effective documentation as efficiently as possible. The forms in Part IV of this book will help you compile the information you need for your documentation project. When you fill them out, you are actually creating a basic documentation plan. In some circumstances, however, you may need to create a documentation plan that is more formal. A formal documentation plan contains the following elements:

○ A description of the project

○ A list of existing information that will help you write the documentation

○ A definition of the goals for each manual or other printed piece and for each on-line component

○ A profile (description) of the audience for each document

○ A document description for each printed piece that describes the design (page layout, binding, etc.) and how the piece will be produced

○ A list of the people working on each document, the tasks they are responsible for, and how to contact them

This chapter contains an explanation of each of these elements and a sample documentation plan to answer any further questions you may have about how to develop them. (Chapter 8, "Types of Documentation," describes the different types of documentation and explains how to decide which ones you need.)

DESCRIBING THE PROJECT

You need an overview of the project. A product manager or systems analyst may have provided you with one at the beginning of the project. If not, write an overview using information from interviews, programmer's notes, or, if they are available, the functional specifications. The overview should include descriptions of the following:

○ General purpose of the software

○ Intended users of the software

○ Features of the software

○ Features that are outstanding or that make it superior to other similar software

○ Documentation for the project, outlining the different printed and on-line documents

○ Number of disks and what they will contain

○ Operating system and other related software

○ Computer and other related hardware

○ Network or larger system the software may be part of

LOCATING EXISTING INFORMATION

You want to gather as much existing information as possible, not only to make sure your documentation is complete but also to save yourself from reinventing the proverbial wheel. This information might include some or all of the following:

○ Software specifications

○ Document specifications

○ Requirements definitions

○ Design analyses

○ Previous published versions of the document

○ Previous drafts of the document completed by other writers

○ Notes made by someone who has worked on, or is working on, the project

○ Diagrams, flow charts, etc.

People are resources too. List the individuals who might have helpful information, such as

○ your supervisor (or the person who gave you the assignment)

○ programmers

○ marketing personnel

○ experts in the field (for example, accountants for a spreadsheet or drafters for a computer-aided design program)

○ writers who have worked on similar documents on the same subject

DEFINING DOCUMENTATION GOALS

Define the scope and objectives of each printed or on-line document. Answer such questions as

○ Is the document a teaching tool or a reference?

○ Do you want the users to learn only the basics or to become experts?

○ Do you want the users to become experts with all functions of the software or only with some?

○ Should the users reach a novice or intermediate level of expertise in preparation for learning more advanced skills?

WRITING AN AUDIENCE PROFILE

An audience profile helps you decide what type of documents and how many you need, how to organize the documentation, and what level of technicality to use in the language in each document. To create your audience profile,

- identify the group or groups of users who will read your document

- write descriptions of each group

- if you have more than one group, decide which are primary users and which are secondary

IDENTIFYING THE AUDIENCE

To identify the users, name each identifiable group. Users, for instance, may be part of a single group with similar needs and similar backgrounds. They could be, for instance, company managers, accounting personnel, or NC machinists. Frequently, the users may include two or more groups of people. For instance, the users of a spreadsheet program could include both business and home office users. In other instances, such as an audience for a game program, the users may not belong to any single identifiable group.

DESCRIBING THE AUDIENCE

Describe each group in your audience. Include any information that affects the users' response to your documentation, such as

- level of computer expertise

- occupation

- knowledge about the field and the subject

- position in organization or field

- level of education

- age group

- reasons for using the program

CLASSIFYING PRIMARY AND SECONDARY USERS

When your software program will be used by more than one identifiable group, you also need to decide which groups are primary and which are secondary. This classification helps you determine how much weight to give to various types of information.

Often, primary readers are primary simply because they make up a majority. Sometimes, however, the primary group is fewer in number but is the most important because its members are the ones who will be using the software most of the time.

DESCRIBING THE DOCUMENT(S)

In your document plan, you also need to include a physical description of the documentation and how it will be produced. If your documentation is commercially typeset and printed, a set of document specifications may be available. *Specifications* describe the design of the document in precise detail. If possible, get a copy of the specifications, as well as samples of the page layout, and include them in your document plan.

The information in your document description helps you do the following:

○ Create a realistic schedule.

○ Make informed writing decisions. You need to know the length of the document, for instance, to decide how many pages to devote to each subject, and you need to know if you can use tables, multiple columns, and extensive formatting to present information.

○ Determine who's responsible for each of the tasks involved.

If you have to design and produce the document, see Chapter 3, "Designing a Document."

A SIMPLE DOCUMENT DESCRIPTION

If your document is produced in-house with a word processor and a photocopy machine, your description will be fairly simple and would include

- estimated length in pages
- number of copies required
- the type of word processing program to be used
- an illustration or an excerpt from an existing document showing the correct page layout (margins, line spacing, indentations, etc.)
- guidelines on how to format headings and words that need special emphasis
- a description of the binding

A COMPLEX DOCUMENT DESCRIPTION

If your document is more complex and you're using more sophisticated production methods, your description would include

- estimated length in pages
- number of copies required
- pages printed front, or front and back
- page (or trim) size
- page layout: margins, indentations, line spacing

○ types of graphics (illustrations? charts? tables? screen dumps?)

○ typesetting method (desktop publishing? conventional?)

○ printing or reproduction method (offset? laser printer? Linotronic? photocopy?)

○ production method for illustrations (graphic artists? CAD/CAM equipment? draw or paint program? photocopied from other sources?)

○ method of page make-up (conventional paste-up? page make-up software?)

○ binding (three-ring binder? spiral? perfect?)

○ paper stock

○ type styles and sizes for text, headings, captions, running heads and feet, and special emphasis

○ inks (colors and percentages)

○ special graphic treatments (screens, overlays)

LISTING TEAM MEMBERS

In your documentation plan, include a list of the people involved in the project, their responsibilities, and how to contact them. Team members might include

○ project supervisor

○ programmers

○ product manager

○ technical consultants

- other writers

- editors

- reviewers

- proofreaders

- typists or word processors

- photocopy personnel

- illustrators

- paste-up artists

- desktop publishing specialists

- typesetters

- printers

- collators, assemblers, and binders

SAMPLE DOCUMENTATION PLAN

Here is a sample of a documentation plan.

DOCUMENTATION PLAN FOR <u>LEARNING BLUEPRINT</u>

Project Description:

Blueprint is a CAD/CAM program for microcomputers running MS-DOS or PC-DOS. The program requires an EGA card and 520K memory. The complete Blueprint package contains

Printed materials:
  Installation Guide
  Learning Blueprint Manual
  Blueprint Reference Manual
  Quick Reference Card

Software disks:
   Blueprint Program disk
   Printer Driver disks (2)
   On-line Help disk
   Drawing Sampler disk

Team Members:

Project manager: Suzanne Sullivan, x235
Lead programmer: Maria Velasquez, x241
Product manager: Bette Fields, x502
Writer: Michael Delcourt, x332
Editor: Jon Frederickson, x346
Designer: Li Pu Wu, 202-2351
Production supervisor: Conrad Bailey, x410
Word processing: Felicity Smith, x 557

Sources of Information:

Program specs
Blueprint Reference Manual
Gene Wright, writer of Blueprint Reference Manual

Scope and Objectives:

The Learning Blueprint manual is a tutorial that introduces
new users to the Blueprint CAD/CAM program. They can learn
and practice basic skills using both the mouse and the keyboard.
They will learn how to accomplish basic drawing and revision
tasks and how to use the on-line help system.

After users have read the Learning Blueprint manual and
practiced its exercises, they can easily research options and
learn variations by using the Blueprint Reference Manual.

Audience Profile:

Most users will be experienced drafters, designers, and
engineers, with little or no experience using either
microcomputers or a CAD/CAM program. They want to learn
the basics of drawing, revising, and printing architectural or
engineering plans. The users want to be able to complete
drawings quickly and retrieve, modify, and combine drawings
with ease.

Document Description:

Length: Approximately 150 pages.

Design: 6¾" × 8⅝" pages, printed front and back.

Page layout: Two-column format with sideheads. (See production department for specs.)

Illustrations: Two pages of conceptual art introduce each section. All other art will be screen dumps produced on Blueprint.

Binding: Spiral binding.

Production: Typesetting and layout in-house on desktop publishing system; printed by offset.

Whether your documentation plan is similar to this one or not, it's sure to help you create effective documentation and keep you from straying off course during the project.

CHAPTER 3

Designing a Document

A good design can make a manual more readable and give you, the writer, the means for presenting information clearly and cleanly.

A design for a software manual has to meet two goals: to make it easy for readers to absorb information on the first reading and easy for them to locate specific bits of information later when they may need them. Generally, to design a manual that meets both these requirements, you should do the following:

○ Format the separate elements consistently so readers can identify them at a glance. All procedures should look alike, all examples should look alike, and so on. For example, if you indent one example five spaces and use italic type, format every other example exactly the same way.

O Use a generous amount of *white space* (blank space) on the page. Information stands out on a page with white space, and the pages are less tiring to read.

O Use headings to show the structure and hierarchy of the information. Format them so they stand out from the text and so the subordination is clear.

O Make columns of text no wider than 65 to 70 characters per line (depending on type style and size). An average line should be four to five inches wide. Wider lines of type are hard to read.

If you work with a graphic design firm, they should provide you with a set of specifications. If you design the document yourself, consulting with typesetters, printers, etc., you should record all of the design information yourself. A document specification generally includes

O page or trim size (several pages may be printed on one large piece of paper stock; trim size is the final size of the printed page)

O paper stock, weight, and color

O type styles and sizes

O line spacing, margins, and indentations for text, headings, lists, procedures, warnings, etc.

O placement and presentation of illustrations

O formatting for special text

O placement and format for running heads and running feet

O format for warnings, notes, and cautions

O format for examples

O format for displays of input/output

○ format for chapter and part openings

○ ink (colors and percentages), if applicable

○ description of any screens or other special graphics

○ binding

Sometimes the current version of the software documentation has to be revised or updated. If this possibility exists, your design should allow for the addition, removal, and substitution of revised or updated material. Many software publishers use a page numbering system keyed to the chapter number (1-1, 1-2, 1-3, etc.) rather than one that numbers the entire document sequentially. This numbering scheme, used in combination with a loose-leaf binder, makes it easy for users to insert additional or revised pages. (See Chapter 7, "Corrections, Addenda, and New Versions.")

In this chapter, we'll look first at the simplest types of design projects, where you produce manuals with a word processing program and a photocopy machine. Then we'll look at more challenging projects, where you produce manuals by having them typeset (either commercially or with desktop publishing) and printed by a commercial print shop.

DESIGNING A SIMPLE DOCUMENT

Many in-house manuals are produced with word processing software and photocopy machines. With this method you print out a master copy of the text that includes space for the illustrations. You insert the illustrations into the master copy by either interleafing them among the pages of the text or by pasting them in place. You then use a photocopy machine to reproduce the required number of pages from the master copy.

Usually, the manual will be printed on one side only of standard 8½ × 11 inch paper stock and will be bound in either a loose-leaf notebook or a brad-type binder.

Figure 3.1 (on page 30) illustrates an effective page layout for a simple, inexpensive manual.

DESIGNING A COMMERCIALLY PRODUCED DOCUMENT

If you're using commercial typesetters and print shops to produce your manual, they will be happy to give you advice on typography and layout. A commercial typesetter will often offer design, layout, and paste-up as well as typesetting services and can help you write a set of specifications. If you're using desktop publishing to typeset and make up your pages, the documentation that accompanies the software often includes information on typography and page layout. For more information on design, see the "Resources" appendix at the end of this book for a list of helpful books.

When you use either desktop publishing or commercial typesetting to typeset and lay out your document, you have many design options. You can choose from many different type styles and sizes, and you have great flexibility in page layout.

Typesetting, layout, and printing services use a system of measurement based on points and picas:

1 point = ¹⁄₇₂ inch

12 points = 1 pica

6 picas = roughly 1 inch

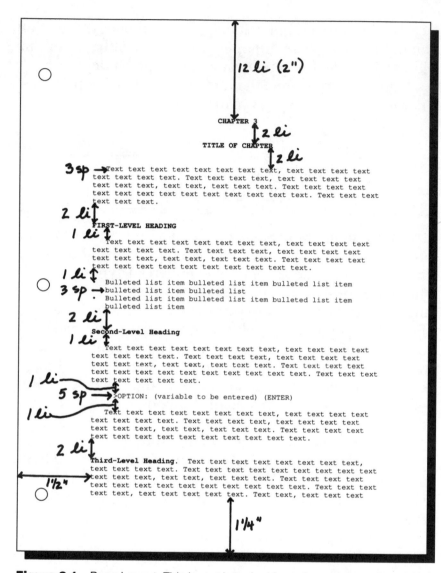

Figure 3.1. Page Layout. This layout is typical for a document produced on a typewriter or with a word processing program. Readers can easily recognize the hierarchy of the headings because of the way they are formatted.

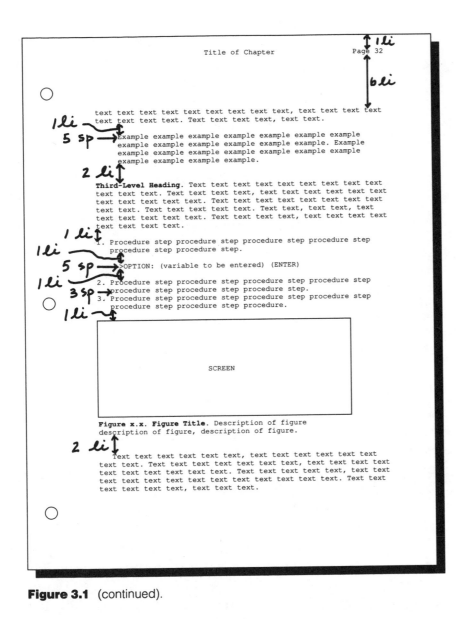

Figure 3.1 (continued).

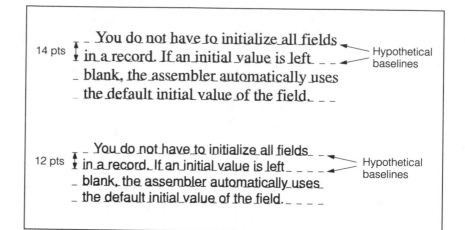

Figure 3.2. Type Specifications. The first example is set in Times Roman 12/14. Times Roman is a serif type style. (*Serifs* are the curves and flourishes on the letters.) The second example is set in Helvetica 10/12. Helvetica is a sans serif type style—that is, a type style without the curves and flourishes. For the main text, a serif type style is considered more readable than a sans serif one.

Type comes in a variety of styles, some common ones being Helvetica, Times Roman, and Bodoni. Courier, standard on most typewriters, is a type style familiar to most of us. Each style can have variations. For instance, Helvetica might be available in Helvetica Light, Helvetica, Helvetica Italic, Helvetica Medium, and Helvetica Bold.

Type is measured in points. Typical type sizes for text are 10, 11, and 12 points. When you specify the type size, you also specify the *leading* (space between lines of type). Leading is typically 2 points greater than the type size. For instance, you might specify 12 on 14 (written *12/14*) Times Roman, meaning the size of the type is 12 points and each line of type is 14 points deep. Leading is measured from baseline to baseline, as illustrated in Figure 3.2.

Headings are usually set in larger sizes, ranging from 14 points to 48 points, and are usually set in a bold typeface that complements the style used for the text.

The text in most manuals is set *ragged right* (with an uneven right margin) rather than *justified* (with straight left and right margins).

Commercially printed manuals are usually printed on the front and back of the page, and a gutter margin is included in the specifications. A *gutter margin* is a margin on the inside of each page large enough to accommodate the binding. On a right-hand page, the gutter margin is on the left, and on a left-hand page, the gutter margin is on the right.

EXAMPLES OF PAGE LAYOUT

Figures 3.3 through 3.6 show how several professional software publishers have used page layout to effectively present information. Even if you don't have all their resources for design and production, you can copy many of their ideas for your manuals. In addition, look through as many software manuals as you can for additional design ideas. For more examples of page layout, see the figures in Part II, which show pages from tutorials, procedures guides, reference manuals, and quick reference materials.

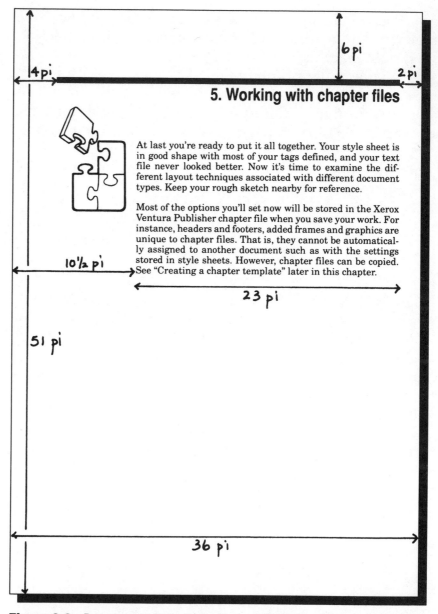

5. Working with chapter files

At last you're ready to put it all together. Your style sheet is in good shape with most of your tags defined, and your text file never looked better. Now it's time to examine the different layout techniques associated with different document types. Keep your rough sketch nearby for reference.

Most of the options you'll set now will be stored in the Xerox Ventura Publisher chapter file when you save your work. For instance, headers and footers, added frames and graphics are unique to chapter files. That is, they cannot be automatically assigned to another document such as with the settings stored in style sheets. However, chapter files can be copied. See "Creating a chapter template" later in this chapter.

Figure 3.3. Page Layout (from *Xerox Ventura Publisher Workbook*). Notice the design of the chapter opening, which has a graphic, a generous amount of white space, and a heavy *rule* (line) setting off the title. On the following pages, lighter-weight rules set off the headings, with two rules setting off major headings and one rule setting off subordinate headings. The manual has a soft cover and ⅝-inch spiral binding (*note:* pi = picas).

↕ 2 pi

Setting the Options menu

Before you start to lay out your chapter file, you should take a look at the Options menu. In this menu are convenience options and program parameters which you can set to make document layout easier. Most of the options are self-explanatory.

For example, if you'll be adding several frames or graphic objects to your chapter file, you probably want to turn on column guides and rulers. If you hide all the pictures files after you've loaded, sized, and cropped them, you'll speed up program operation. By first selecting a frame, you can hide a single picture, rather than all pictures.

One dialog box in particular, Set Preferences, needs more detailed discussion.

Set Preferences

Here are a few suggestions for setting the Set Preferences dialog box to work well with most document types.

➤ Select Set Preferences in the Options menu.

The Set Preferences dialog box displays.

```
┌─────────────────────────────────────────────────┐
│ SET PREFERENCES                              [?] │
│                                                  │
│        Generated Tags:  Hidden      ↕            │
│         Text to Greek:  10          ↕            │
│      Keep Backup Files: Yes         ↕            │
│      Double Click Speed: Fast       ↕            │
│       On-Screen Kerning: None       ↕            │
│       Auto-Adjustments:  Both       ↕            │
│    Pop-Up Menu Symbols:  Shown      ↕            │
│            Menu Type:   Pull-Down ↕              │
│                                                  │
│    Decimal Tab Char:  046  (ASCII)               │
│                                 ┌────┐ ┌──────┐  │
│                                 │ OK │ │Cancel│  │
│                                 └────┘ └──────┘  │
└─────────────────────────────────────────────────┘
```

2 pi ↕

Figure 3.3 (continued).

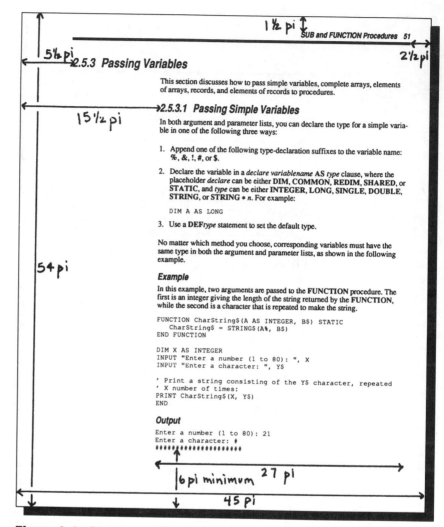

Figure 3.4. Page Layout (from *Microsoft® QuickBASIC*). Generous amounts of white space make the dense technical material easier to read, and numbered headings provide a clear-cut structure. It's easy to see the major heading, which sits to the far left in a larger size of type. Input/output, because it is in a contrasting type style, stands out from the rest of the text. The manual has a soft cover and *perfect* (glued) binding.

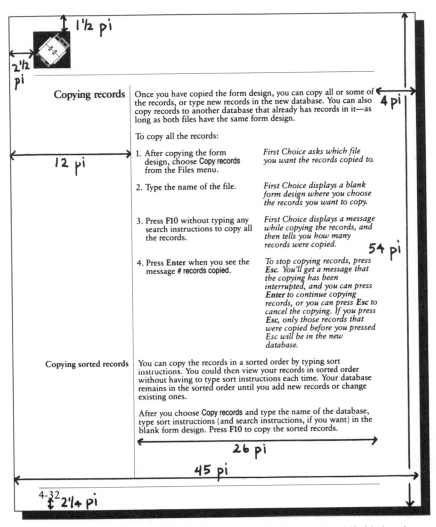

Within the figure:

1½ pi

2½ pi

4 pi

12 pi

54 pi

Copying records

Once you have copied the form design, you can copy all or some of the records, or type new records in the new database. You can also copy records to another database that already has records in it—as long as both files have the same form design.

To copy all the records:

1. After copying the form design, choose Copy records from the Files menu.	*First Choice asks which file you want the records copied to.*
2. Type the name of the file.	*First Choice displays a blank form design where you choose the records you want to copy.*
3. Press **F10** without typing any search instructions to copy all the records.	*First Choice displays a message while copying the records, and then tells you how many records were copied.*
4. Press **Enter** when you see the message # records copied.	*To stop copying records, press **Esc**. You'll get a message that the copying has been interrupted, and you can press **Enter** to continue copying records, or you can press **Esc** to cancel the copying. If you press **Esc**, only those records that were copied before you pressed Esc will be in the new database.*

Copying sorted records

You can copy the records in a sorted order by typing sort instructions. You could then view your records in sorted order without having to type sort instructions each time. Your database remains in the sorted order until you add new records or change existing ones.

After you choose Copy records and type the name of the database, type sort instructions (and search instructions, if you want) in the blank form design. Press **F10** to copy the sorted records.

26 pi

45 pi

4-32　2¼ pi

Figure 3.5. Page Layout (from *PFS: First Choice® Version 3.02*). Notice the two columns, one for headings and one for text, and the narrow rules that structure the page. An icon acts as a running head. The different type sizes of the headings clearly show their hierarchy. Notice the two-column arrangement of the procedure. The manual has a soft cover and perfect binding.

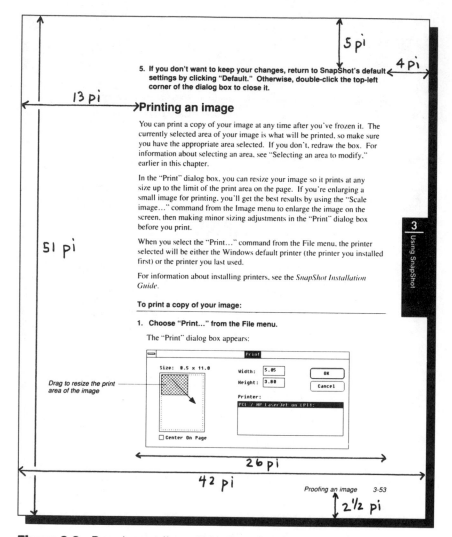

Figure 3.6. Page Layout (from *Aldus SnapShot User Manual*). Readers can easily locate each procedure; the introduction is in bold type and underlined with a narrow rule, and each step in the procedure is also in bold type. In this particular procedure, a screen illustrates the first step. Any callouts for the illustrations sit in the wide left margin. The chapter number and title are in reverse type on a colored tab, demarcations that make chapters easy to find. The manual has a soft cover and ½-inch spiral binding.

CHAPTER 4

Planning the Illustrations

Procedures tell users what to do and how to do it, but illustrations *show* them. Illustrations can include screen dumps, diagrams, charts, tables, drawings, icons, and photographs; they all help you clarify explanations, descriptions, and procedures. They're invaluable for showing users what's happening on the computer screen at critical points. Besides supporting and clarifying the text, illustrations break up intimidating blocks of technical information to make your manual look more interesting, more . . . human.

When you're planning illustrations for your documentation, you need to consider the following:

○ Resources. Do you have the materials, equipment, and personnel necessary to produce the illustrations and the design?

○ Cost. Will the cost of the illustrations and the design fall within your budget?

○ Schedule. Can you produce the illustrations and the design within the time available?

MAKING A PRELIMINARY LIST

Begin planning your illustrations early. If you're using illustrations that must be produced by a graphics department, you may need to make a preliminary list of them before you complete the first draft. If you're producing most of the illustrations yourself with screen dumps, you might list the illustrations while you're writing the first draft or even later, when it's completed. Use the following method to make a preliminary list of illustrations:

○ Go through the outline or the draft, chapter by chapter, locating every explanation, description, and procedure that needs an illustration.

○ Give each illustration a title. (When you finalize the list, you'll also give each one a number.) You may or may not use the title in the manual, but you'll definitely need it as a tag for production purposes.

○ Indicate the type of illustration needed and its probable size.

○ Indicate which illustrations are optional—that is, which illustrations are desirable but not actually necessary.

Because production methods for tables differ from those used for illustrations, make a separate list of tables for each chapter.

As you are writing the first draft, you'll revise the list—changing, adding, or subtracting illustrations—and decide which of the optional illustrations to include in the manual. To help you coordinate the production of the art, number the illustrations using a system based on chapter numbers (3-1, 3-2, 3-3, etc.). Give a copy of the final list of illustrations to the department or graphics firm that is laying out and pasting up the manual.

Here's an example of a preliminary list of illustrations for a chapter in a desktop publishing manual. The writer put parentheses around the descriptions of the optional illustrations; you might tag them some other way.

CHAPTER 3: WORKING WITH TEXT AND PICTURE FILES

No.	Title & Description	Size	Type
3.1	Chapter 3 opening. Concept art— typing manual in wastebasket?	2″ (in margin)	Line art
3.2	Properly Formatted File.	1 page	Create with program & print
3.3	Tagging Text Files. (Piece of sculpted text with tag?)	2″ (in margin)	Line art
3.4	Tags in a Document.	1 page	Create
3.5	Creating Text Files. (Boy about to chop down tree?)	6″ (in margin)	Line art
3.6	Line Art File. Probably a bar chart.	2″ (in margin)	Create
3.7	Image File. Scanned photo?	2″ (in margin)	Create
3.8	Gray Scale. For scanning section.	2″ (in margin)	Line art
3.9	Directory of Files with Proper Names.	½ page	Screen dump

When you're numbering only the line art in your documentation but not the screen dumps, list the screen dumps separately. You should also give them numbers which can be used solely for production purposes (S-3.1, S-3.2, S-3.3, for instance).

USING CAPTIONS

Many illustrations will appear immediately after the definitions, descriptions, or procedures they are supporting. When this is the case, you may choose not to title or number the illustrations. Often, however, illustrations must have numbers to help readers locate them. For instance, an illustration may appear at some distance from the material it supports. Or you may need to refer to an illustration elsewhere in the text. In these cases, even if you decide not to title the illustrations, you must number them. Use a numbering system keyed to chapter numbers (Figure 1-1, Figure 1-2, Figure 1-3, etc. in Chapter 1). Titles are optional.

For instance, you might number and title the illustrations in Chapters 1 and 2 like this:

Figure 1.1. A Sample Menu.
Figure 1.2. The Mouse.
Figure 2.1. Choosing a Command.
Figure 2.2. Filling in a Command Field.

A caption for a figure usually appears immediately below the illustration, flush left. A caption for a table usually appears above the table, flush left, but can also appear directly below it. Whichever position you choose, use it consistently. You can see examples of how software publishers typically handle captions in the illustrations in this chapter.

SCREEN SHOTS (SCREEN DUMPS)

The most useful illustrations, of course, are representations of the computer screen. The most common method of creating this type of illustration is with the screen shot or, as it is often called, the screen dump. The software for dumping a screen has improved greatly, allowing you to set up your screens and print them out on a laser printer to produce high-quality illustrations. There are dozens of software programs available today for screen dumping. You're limited, of course, to those that work with your software and your printer.

Figures 4.1 and 4.2 show examples of screen shots.

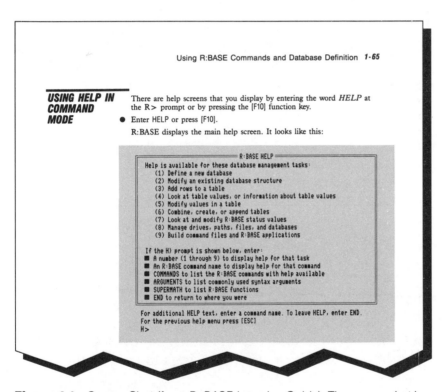

Figure 4.1. Screen Shot (from *R: BASE Learning Guide*). The screen shot is set off with a *screen tint* (a shaded area created by printing with dots so ink coverage is less than 100 percent). When the screen shot has no border or frame, you can use an overlay or, more commonly, a border in the shape of a computer screen.

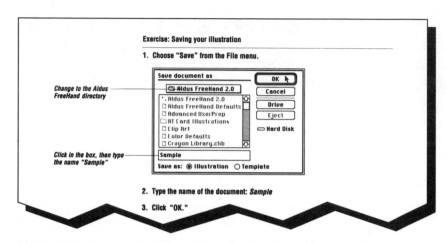

Figure 4.2. Screen Shot (from *Aldus FreeHand User Manual*). This screen shot has *callouts*, descriptive comments tied to elements in the illustration with lines or arrows.

DIAGRAMS AND DRAWINGS

Diagrams and drawings add interest to software manuals and make them easier to read. You can use a diagram to show readers the steps in a procedure and the stages of a process or to help them visualize objects, such as parts or elements. Figures 4.3 through 4.5 are examples.

Drawings can help you get concepts across, supporting your descriptions and explanations. Figures 4.6 and 4.7 show how writers have used drawings to enliven their software manuals.

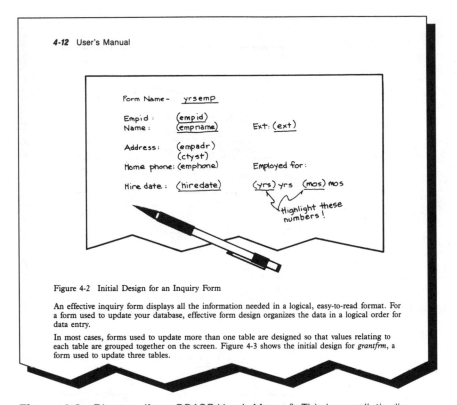

4-12 User's Manual

Form Name – yrsemp

Empid : (empid)
Name : (empname)   Ext: (ext)

Address: (empadr)
         (ctyst)
Home phone: (emphone)   Employed for:

Hire date : (hiredate)   (yrs) yrs   (mos) mos

Highlight these numbers!

Figure 4-2   Initial Design for an Inquiry Form

An effective inquiry form displays all the information needed in a logical, easy-to-read format. For a form used to update your database, effective form design organizes the data in a logical order for data entry.

In most cases, forms used to update more than one table are designed so that values relating to each table are grouped together on the screen. Figure 4-3 shows the initial design for *grantfrm*, a form used to update three tables.

Figure 4.3. Diagram (from *RBASE User's Manual*). This is a realistic diagram of how a user might design a form. Notice the caption below the figure, which includes the figure number and title.

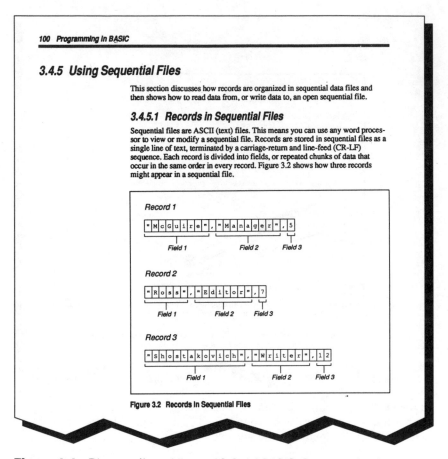

Figure 4.4. Diagram (from *Microsoft® QuickBASIC: Programming in BASIC*). This diagram illustrates a concept that users might have a hard time visualizing.

Command Dictionary **CD-139**

RULES

```
┌──────────────────────── SYNTAX ────────────────────────┐
│ RULES                                                   │
└─────────────────────────────────────────────────────────┘
```

To define rules by comparison of a column to a constant value:

```
┌──────────────────────────── SYNTAX ────────────────────────────┐
│                              EQ              AND                 │
│                              NE              OR                  │
│                              GT         value  AND NOT          │
│   "message"   colname        GE              OR NOT             │
│                     IN tblname   LT     value                    │
│                              LE                                 │
│                              CONTAINS                           │
└─────────────────────────────────────────────────────────────────┘
```

"message" is an error message of up to 40 characters
colname is the column whose entry rules are being defined
tblname is the table in which the column is defined (omit to allow the rule to apply to all tables in which the column is defined)

Figure 4.5. Diagram (from *R:BASE Command Dictionary*). You may need to diagram the syntax of commands for your users.

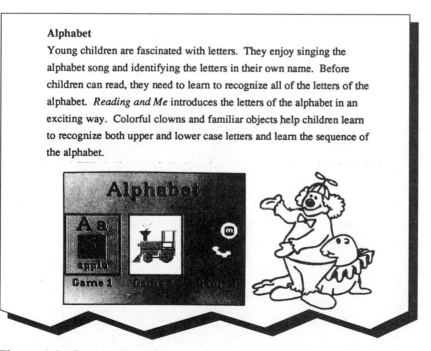

Alphabet

Young children are fascinated with letters. They enjoy singing the alphabet song and identifying the letters in their own name. Before children can read, they need to learn to recognize all of the letters of the alphabet. *Reading and Me* introduces the letters of the alphabet in an exciting way. Colorful clowns and familiar objects help children learn to recognize both upper and lower case letters and learn the sequence of the alphabet.

Figure 4.6. Drawing (from *Reading and Me*). A light-hearted drawing suitable for the manual's audience.

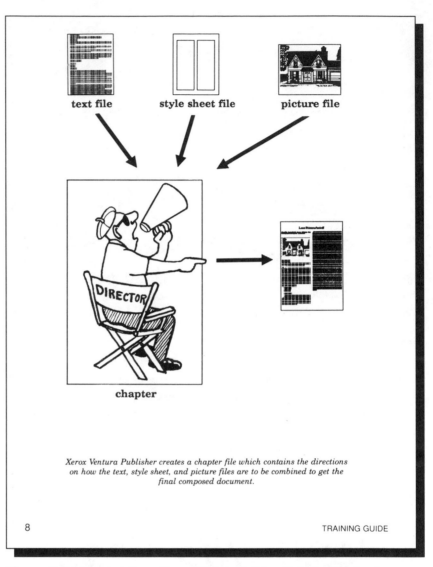

text file   style sheet file   picture file

DIRECTOR

chapter

Xerox Ventura Publisher creates a chapter file which contains the directions on how the text, style sheet, and picture files are to be combined to get the final composed document.

Figure 4.7. Drawing (from *Xerox Ventura Training Guide*). This drawing explains a concept in an effective and entertaining way.

CHARTS

Charts present data graphically to readers, showing proportions and relationships in a way that text alone cannot.

Flow charts are especially helpful in software documentation, as you can see in Figures 4.8 and 4.9.

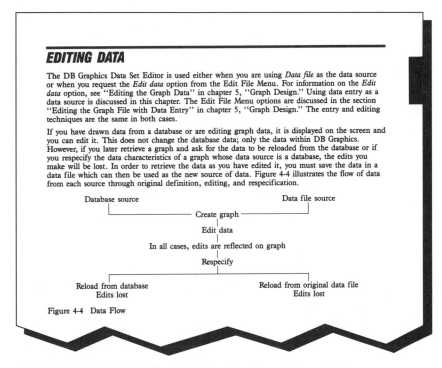

Figure 4.8. Flow Chart (from *DB Graphics User's Manual*). This chart shows users the flow of data in a database.

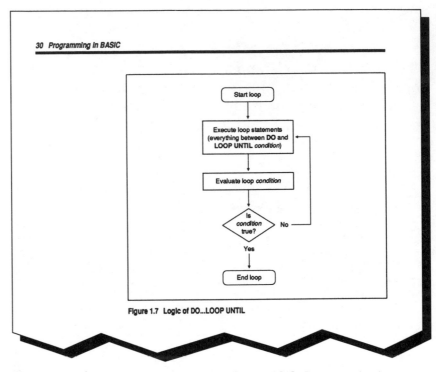

Figure 4.9.   Flow Chart (from *Microsoft QuickBASIC: Programming in BASIC*). This flow chart explains programming logic.

TABLES

You can use tables to lay out data for easy reference, to display data in exact quantities, or to compare large amounts of information.

Here are some guidelines for creating a table:

○ Keep it simple; don't have so many rows or columns that the table becomes hard to read.

○ Space the items for easy reading; avoid both crowding them and spacing them too far apart.

○ Use the vertical columns for your data, not the horizontal rows.

○ Label each column.

○ Keep the table on one page. If it's too big to fit on one page, divide the information into two or more tables. If you have to break a table between pages, be sure to repeat the column headings on the next page.

Tables can be simple, as in Figure 4.10. But often, you'll have more complex information to present. Figure 4.11 illustrates the format for a complex table, and Figure 4.12 is an example of a complex table.

Examples of wildcard templates:

Wildcard filename	Meaning
.	Match any file name and extension (default)
*.WKS	Match any file with a .WKS extension
A*.*	Match any file starting with A
A??.*	Match any 3 character name starting with A
*.	Match any name with no extension
?x*.?x*	Match any name with X as the second letter of the name and the second letter of the extension
MYFILE.TXT	Match only the specified file (no wildcard)

Figure 4.10. A Simple Table (from *Rapid Relay User Manual*).

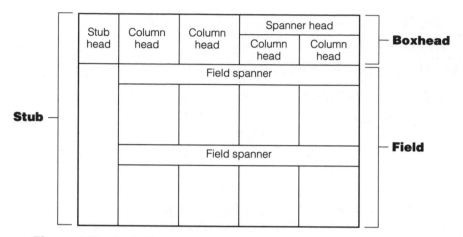

Figure 4.11. Table Format.

Figure 4.12. A Complex Table (from *RBASE for DOS Building Applications/Command Dictionary*).

ICONS

If your program is graphically oriented and uses icons, it's helpful to the readers to include them in your text. They catch the eye and lead readers to the relevant material instantly. Figure 4.13 shows you an effective way to use them. Each icon was defined, of course, earlier in the manual.

PHOTOGRAPHS

Photographs are also an option for illustrating your manual. If you're dealing with hardware installation, a photograph can't be beat, as Figure 4.14 shows.

EXERCISE 1 - LEARNING THE BASICS

Loading a text file

You're ready to start working on a document. First you'll select the frame where you want the text file to appear. In this case, you'll use the page frame that is automatically set up in the working area.

To select a frame:

➤ Select ⊡ Frame mode (i.e., the left mode icon) by moving the mouse cursor over the icon and clicking the mouse button. (Remember, click the left button on a multi-button mouse.)

The frame mode icon will turn black with white lines to indicate it has been enabled (selected).

Small black boxes will appear on the outside edges of the working area to indicate that the page frame has

EXERCISE 6 · MODIFYING A STYLE SHEET

To specify that the height of the Ruling Line will be one quarter of an inch:

➤ Select Height of Rule 1, and enter the amount: 0.250.

➤ Select Space Below Rule 3 and enter the amount: 0.230. Then select ⊡ . This will move the shaded line so it is displayed on top of the text.

➤ Select OK

Shading will be displayed across the line.

You just created a new tag by initially using the attributes set in the Address tag and then by making changes to alignment and ruling line above to produce the effect you see on the screen. This tag could now be applied to other paragraphs.

20

Figure 4.13. Icons (from *Xerox Ventura Training Guide*). Icons catch the eye, showing the user what to select.

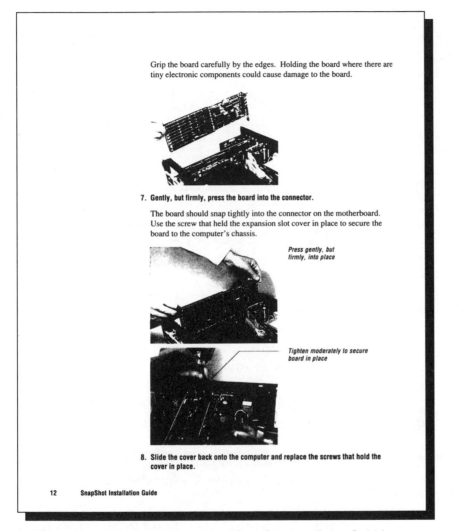

Grip the board carefully by the edges. Holding the board where there are tiny electronic components could cause damage to the board.

7. Gently, but firmly, press the board into the connector.

The board should snap tightly into the connector on the motherboard. Use the screw that held the expansion slot cover in place to secure the board to the computer's chassis.

Press gently, but firmly, into place

Tighten moderately to secure board in place

8. Slide the cover back onto the computer and replace the screws that hold the cover in place.

12   SnapShot Installation Guide

Figure 4.14. Photographs (from *Aldus SnapShot Installation Guide*).

CHAPTER 5

Setting Standards

Just as programmers strive for clean and elegant code in software, writers strive for clean and elegant language in documents. A style guide can help you set standards that make your documents readable and give them a professional polish.

A *style guide* is a compendium of guidelines on spelling, punctuation, and usage. A style guide

○ ensures consistency between what the readers see on the computer screen and what they see on the printed page

○ helps eliminate inconsistencies and small errors that confuse and distract readers

○ helps coordinate the effort between team members, including reviewers, writers, editors, and proofreaders

○ makes the job of writing easier because you can find the information you need in one easy-to-use reference

If your organization doesn't have its own official style guide, create one containing guidelines for

- conventions to be used in the manual
- terminology
- spelling
- abbreviations
- numbers and symbols
- punctuation

Even if your organization has an official style guide, you need to compile guidelines for the terms, symbols, and usages in your specific document.

In addition, you should have on hand

- one of the standard manuals on style, such as *The Chicago Manual of Style* or *Words into Type*
- a good dictionary
- a book on grammar

If you're involved in documenting software for the United States government, you'll probably use *The Government Printing Office Style Manual*. See the "Resources" appendix at the end of this book for some additional suggestions.

The sections that follow will help you decide what you need to include in your style guide. You can see a sample style guide at the end of the chapter.

TERMINOLOGY

You may be writing a draft for a new manual and find that a certain object, process, or concept has two or three different names. For instance, the word *terminal* may appear in one place and the word *work station* in another, when both terms refer to the same piece of equipment. And although the meaning may be perfectly clear to you, you can confuse readers by using *disk* and *diskette* interchangeably.

Select the simplest term and use it consistently throughout your document. You add confusion, not variety, when you use two or three terms to refer to the same thing. If readers need to know both terms, provide definitions for both.

Remember, you want terminology to be the same on both the computer screen and in the documentation so users won't be confused. Also be sure to reserve those words that refer to specific objects or concepts and avoid using them in their more general meanings. For instance, you might reserve for specific use words such as

function	record
system	field
backup	file

CONVENTIONS

You'll want to emphasize certain terms in your manuals so your readers can recognize them instantly, including

- ○ commands
- ○ command options
- ○ key names
- ○ text to be typed by the user

For instance, you might put all command names in full capital letters, like this:

Select the FIND command from the menu.

In addition, you also need to establish a style for instructing readers to take action. For instance, when you direct them to use the keyboard to type in a filename, will you write "*Type* the filename" or "*Enter* the filename"?

Typically, you'll instruct readers to

- ○ type or enter text from the keyboard (*Type LET A-3*)
- ○ press individual keys (*Press ENTER* or *Press the Enter key*)
- ○ press combinations of keys (*Press Alt-A, Press Alt + A,* or *Hold down the Alt key and press A*).

For your readers' convenience, list the conventions you're using in the front of your manual. The sample style guide at the end of this chapter shows one way to emphasize such text. (Examples of "Symbols and Conventions" appear in Chapter 9, "The Parts of a Document.")

SPELLING

Your style guide should show you how to spell, hyphenate, and capitalize the following types of words:

○ Company and product names

○ Problem words

○ Technical terms

COMPANY AND PRODUCT NAMES

Find out the official spelling of any company and product names that you'll be mentioning in the document. Be specific; copy the capitalization, the abbreviations, the spacing, and the punctuation exactly. It may seem obvious to you, but your readers can't be sure that Bizitime Forms, Inc. is the same as BusyTime Forms Co. Don't write *A.B.C. Co.* when their letterhead says *The ABC Company*. And if their product is spelled Inter Form, don't write Interform. You not only risk confusing your readers, you risk offending the organization as well.

Remember also that there are copyright laws. You may have to use a copyright symbol with a company name or a registered trademark symbol with a product name the first time you mention either of them in your document. Your supervisor or your organization's legal department should be able to give you guidelines.

PROBLEM WORDS

Certain words, like *accommodate* and *unnecessary,* consistently give writers trouble. Look up the correct spelling of any potentially troublesome words and add them to your style guide.

Words specific to the computer field also give writers trouble. Do you write *database* or *data base*? *Filename* or *file name*?

For words that have more than one correct spelling, decide which spelling to use. For instance, you could use either *indexes* or *indices* as the plural for the word *index.*

ACRONYMS AND ABBREVIATIONS

Spell out each acronym the first time you mention it. If your document is long, however, you may need to spell out an acronym the first time you use it in each chapter or major subdivision.

FIRST MENTION OF AN ACRONYM:

The simulation includes instrumentation as specified by the Federal Aviation Administration (FAA).

SUBSEQUENT MENTION OF AN ACRONYM:

For more information, read the <u>Flight Training Handbook</u> published by the FAA.

Spell out each abbreviation the first time you use it or, in a longer document, the first time you use it in each major division.

FIRST MENTION OF AN ABBREVIATION:

The resolution is measured in dots per inch (dpi).

SUBSEQUENT MENTION OF AN ABBREVIATION:

The printer gives you 300 dpi in draft mode.

If your document uses acronyms and abbreviations extensively, list them in the front matter for your readers' convenience.

NUMBERS AND SYMBOLS

Your document may make extensive use of numbers and symbols, perhaps setting out mathematical equations or scientific notation.

In most technical documents, quantities such as distance, length, area, volume, and so on are given in figures (2), whereas in ordinary text they are spelled out (two).

In your style guide, include the rules you want to use in your document, clarifying them with examples. For instance, your style guide might include the following:

EXAMPLES OF NUMBER STYLE:

640K	90%
2D, 3D	8K-bps rate
3 cubic feet	10°30′
6 meters	12 V
3″ × 5″	the ratio 0.75

You should also spell out rules for using special emphasis in displays of numbers and symbols. For instance, you may italicize variables in an equation or give them some other kind of special emphasis.

PUNCTUATING A SERIES

Insert a comma after the next to the last item (before *and* or *or*) in the series.

EXAMPLES OF A COMMA IN A SERIES:

The total should equal Actual Frame Width after you've entered all margin, column, and gutter widths.

Use inches, centimeters, or fractional points as your unit of measure.

HANDLING PROCEDURES

Decide how to handle the punctuation and capitalization for procedures. Here are some guidelines:

- O Conclude the introductory statement with a colon (:).
- O Capitalize the first letter in each step.
- O Conclude each step with a period (.).

EXAMPLE OF A PROCEDURE:

Use the reserved glossary name "footnote" if you accidentally delete an automatic footnote number in the footnote window. To insert the footnote glossary:

1. Type <u>footnote</u> at the location in the footnote window where you need to insert the footnote number.
2. Expand the glossary by holding down the Command key while pressing the Backspace key.

HANDLING LISTS

No matter how you decide to capitalize and punctuate your lists, consistency is vital. Although styles vary, one of the simplest and most common methods is to end the introductory statement with a colon and to capitalize the first letter of each list item, with a period at the end of each list item being optional. Here's an example:

The six stages in organizing your General Ledger records are:

1. Determining the layout of the financial statements
2. Classifying accounts
3. Assigning account numbers
4. Identifying integration accounts
5. Suppressing zero balances
6. Ensuring that debits and credits balance

You can choose from a number of different styles. The following guidelines for punctuating and capitalizing lists are from *The Chicago Manual of Style*.

When the introductory statement to a list is a complete sentence, then

- ○ conclude the statement with either a period (.) or a colon (:)

- ○ capitalize the first letter in each item and end it with a period when the items are complete sentences

- ○ don't capitalize the first letter of each item (nor end it with a period) when the items are single words, phrases, or sentence fragments

Here's an example where the introductory statement is a complete sentence ending with a period:

This chapter is important for several reasons.
- ○ You find out how to get the most out of the training materials.
- ○ You discover three different ways to create a document.
- ○ You learn how to create typographic effects.

In the next example, the introductory statement is a complete sentence ending with a colon.

You can choose from several units of measure:
- ○ inches
- ○ centimeters
- ○ picas and points
- ○ fractional points

When the introductory statement says that information will follow, however, then conclude the statement with a colon (:). Here's an example:

Create a new division when you want to do one of the following:
- ○ Change the page number style.
- ○ Change the position of the page number.
- ○ Change the page numbering sequence.

When the introductory statement is an incomplete sentence that each list item completes, then

- ○ end the statement without punctuation

- ○ don't capitalize the first letter in each item, and don't end it with a period

Here's an example:

Create a new division when you want to
- ○ change the page number style
- ○ change the position of the page number
- ○ change the page numbering sequence

HANDLING CAPTIONS

Illustrations, charts, graphs, photographs, and tables in your text will often have identifying numbers and *captions* (titles). Occasionally, an illustration will need a *legend* (explanation) as well. Here are the rules for punctuating captions and legends for illustrations:

○ End the figure number with a period.

○ End the caption (title) with a period.

○ Capitalize the first and last word in the caption and all other words except articles (a, an, the), conjunctions (and, or, for), and prepositions (of, with, what, in, etc.).

○ Punctuate the legend as you would any normal sentence.

You can place the caption and legend either directly above or directly below the illustration. Here's an example:

Figure 3.5. First Step in Newspaper Layout. Here you create the underlying grid with the Margins & Columns command.

SAMPLE STYLE GUIDE

Here's a sample of a style guide created for use in writing a variety of application manuals.

CONVENTIONS

Commands	Use **DESK MENU** to bring up the menu.
Options to be chosen	Choose **Bring to Front**.
Keys to be pressed	Press **Ctrl-A**
Text to be entered	When SmartGuide prompts you for the path, type: A:\HPLJPLUS*.*

SPELLING AND ABBREVIATIONS

adapter

analog

AT

BASIC

bit (K bit, kilobit, 8K-bps rate)

byte (K byte, kilobyte, 28MS bytes, 720K-byte diskdrive, 10M Bps)

CADDS 3

CADDS 4X

CBT

compatible

Computervision

CPU

criteria (plural)

criterion (singular)

data (plural)

datum (singular)

data bank

data base

data link

data processing

data set

default drive

Diconix 150P

disk controller

diskettes

filename

gauge (not guage or gage)

hard copy

hardware

IBM

input, inputting

interact

interpro

Intergraph Corporation

label, labeling, labeled

MACH 20

mainframe

microcomputer

megabytes

Micro D

MS DOS

NEC Multispeed ELX

NEC Multispeed HD

NEC Multispeed LCD

O/S

OEM (singular)

OEMs (plural)

OMEGA

on line (Is the program on line?)

on-line (on-line documentation)

OS/2

PC Works

plotting

queue, queuing

RAM

refer, referring, referred

reference

retrieval

Spell command

upward (not upwards)

Windows

workstation

GUIDELINES

Hyphenate adjectives in front of the word they modify.
   out-of-pocket cost
   double-disk drive

Spell out an acronym on first mention.
   Original Equipment Manufacturer (OEM)

Use lower case for time designations.
   7:00 am; 7:30 pm

NUMBERS AND SYMBOLS

640K

Spell out percent, and, at, and number rather than using %, &, @, and #.
   90 percent, trial and error,
   five at $6.00 each, the number of runs

Spell out numbers ten and under.
   The fight went three rounds.

Use numerals for numbers over ten.
   They completed 30 versions.

Use numerals when a sentence includes numbers both under and over ten.
   She needed 3 copies of each of the 15 documents.

For very large numbers:
   The series included 20 million items.

PUNCTUATION

Put a comma before and or or in a series of three or more.
   You can choose one option, all options, or no options.

This is an example of the correct way to punctuate lists:
   Keep the following objectives in mind:

   O Information must be accurate.

   O Information must be timely.

   O Information must be applicable.

REFERENCES

The Chicago Manual of Style
Webster's Dictionary

CHAPTER 6

Reviews, Usability Tests, and Revisions

Reviewers can point out areas that need clarification, information that you've left out, and mistakes. The complexity of the documentation dictates the number of reviews you need. For a simple software program with a brief manual, you may need only one. For a more complex software program with more documentation, you'll need at least two reviews, one at the time of the beta test and a second one when the manual is finished, before it goes to production. In some cases, when the project is a very complex one, you may need multiple reviews.

The goals of any review are to

○ correct technical inaccuracies

○ check clarity and completeness of explanations and procedures

○ check writing style, terminology, and narrative flow

Your reviewers, therefore, may include programmers, editors, proofreaders, your supervisor, marketing people, and anyone else who can help you meet those goals. You may also conduct separate reviews, each with a different goal. For instance, you might have one review for technical accuracy and one for writing style.

GUIDELINES FOR CONDUCTING A REVIEW

The guidelines for planning a review are the following:

○ Make your review timely. Give reviewers enough time to do a thorough job and yourself enough time to make corrections.

○ When your document is long, divide it into sections and review each section as it's completed.

○ Notify reviewers in advance; tell them the date the draft will arrive and the date they should return it.

PREPARING THE REVIEW DRAFT

To prepare the review draft,

○ be sure the draft is as complete and as error-free as possible

○ put photocopies of any illustrations or rough sketches in place (immediately following the pages that contain the references)

○ note any errors or omissions that you're aware of, marking the location and describing the error or omission

EXAMPLE OF NOTE IN DRAFT:

Chapter 5, "How to Change Colors on Your Screen." Not written yet due to lack of a final decision from programming about the user interface design. Will be included in next review.

Figure 9.1. Drawing of Left-Side Gizmo with callouts to x, y, and z. Art not ready yet. Will be included in next review.

○ make copies for all reviewers, a copy for yourself, and one or two extra copies

WRITING A COVER SHEET

A cover sheet for a review should include the following:

○ The date you handed out the review copies. (You may need "proof" of the date you started the review.)

○ A list of the reviewers. Reviewers may want to confer with one another, and they can also tell you if you've left anyone off the list.

○ A description of the document or the sections of the document being reviewed.

○ Instructions to the reviewers. Be precise. If you want them to pay special attention to certain sections, let them know. If, at an early stage, you want them to review content only and ignore writing style, tell them that too. (You may need to add specific notes for individual reviewers.) Tell them how and where to indicate corrections and make comments.

○ The date they must return the review copy and where to send it.

EXAMPLE OF A COVER SHEET:

Date: July 13, 1989
To: Constance Sukai
     John Baxter
     Linda Ramirez
     Elizabeth Porter
From: Phyllis Rivers

Contents for First Review:
Operator's Manual, Part I, "Setting Up the Machine," and Part II,
"Basic Operation."

Please note that the positions of figures are marked with a
boxed "X" labeled with the figure number. Copies of the figures
for each section are included at the end of the section.

You will receive "Part III, Troubleshooting," and "Part IV,
Specialized Functions," for review on September 1.

Instructions:
Please read all text and check figures for the enclosed material.
I would like you to pay special attention to Chapter 4 as this
describes the most complicated and newest operations. Please
mark corrections or write comments in red on the appropriate
pages and tag each marked page with a paper clip at the top.

Deadline:
Return this copy to Phyllis Rivers by 5:00 pm on July 26.

EVALUATING REVIEWERS' COMMENTS

Straightforward corrections of errors are easy to handle.
However, three types of reviewers' comments deserve special consideration: misunderstandings, editorial comments,
and disagreements.

MISUNDERSTANDINGS.   A misunderstanding occurs when
a reviewer corrects something that isn't wrong or makes a
comment that doesn't seem to make any sense. Although
you may be tempted to ignore these comments, they do

point out problems in the text. If one reader didn't understand what you were saying, others may not either. Read the text over and see if you can make your meaning clearer.

If the text still seems clear to you after looking it over again, take time to discuss the comment with the reviewer. You may gain a new perspective on the problem.

EDITORIAL COMMENTS.   Editorial comments can be vague, sarcastic, or sometimes even offensive. For the good of the document, look for the reason behind the comment.

As with misunderstandings, try to find out the reasons for any offensive or vague comments you don't understand.

DISAGREEMENTS.   If you have several reviewers, you'll eventually run into a disagreement about how a topic is handled or whether it should be handled at all. As the writer, it's up to you to settle these disagreements and decide on the content of your document.

Rank will often make the difference when reviewers disagree. In these cases, you rewrite to suit the person holding most authority as far as your document is concerned.

In other cases, you have to negotiate. Talk to each person individually. Be positive when you introduce the subject. If you prefer one suggestion, state your preference and ask for the reviewer's reaction: "I thought I would rewrite this to say . . . Would that be okay with you?"

If you can't get an agreement, ask the reviewers to meet for a discussion. You may uncover new information and be able to work out a compromise.

No matter how a dispute is resolved, make a note about how and why you reached a decision on it, so that you'll have a record.

HANDLING MULTIPLE REVIEW COPIES

If you have to go through several review copies, do it methodically to save time and effort.

○ Mark all corrections on your master copy.

○ Don't make any changes in the document until you've gone through all the review copies.

○ Read the comments from the most important reviewers first. Usually, these will be your technical experts and your supervisor or project leader.

○ Check off each correction or comment in the review copies as you go through them.

○ Keep in mind that changes in one section may affect other sections. Mark the other sections immediately or make a note to yourself to do so.

○ Initial and date each review copy. You will then be able to tell each reviewer exactly when you read the comments in the review copy.

MANAGING CORRECTIONS AFTER A REVIEW

Mark all corrections on your master copy. To make corrections and revisions, follow these guidelines:

○ Work from your marked-up master copy.

○ Check off the corrections on the master copy as you retype them. If someone else types for you, check the new version against the marked-up master copy.

○ Ask yourself, as you make each correction, if the correction needs to be made in other places or if it affects other parts of your document.

○ Check the text around each correction to see that transitions are correct and in place.

TESTING FOR USABILITY

The best type of review comes from the users themselves. If you have the opportunity, you should test the documentation's usability. Nothing enables you to zero in on omissions and weaknesses so accurately as usability testing. Be prepared for some big surprises. It can be quite painful to watch someone fumbling through what you thought were clear and lucid procedures, growing more and more frustrated as the moments pass. It is also very illuminating. If you have any team members who believe that documentation is not really that important, be sure to include them as observers.

Ordinarily, a usability test of the documentation is conducted during beta testing, when the software is stable and in a user-friendly state. Here's how to plan a usability test:

○ Find volunteers who match your audience profile. You can reward them for their trouble with a free copy of the software program.

○ Write an instruction sheet, listing simple tasks for the volunteers to perform. The tasks should use basic and representative functions of the software.

○ Decide on a reasonable length of time to give the volunteers to complete each exercise.

○ Choose observers from as wide a range of people as possible, including programmers, marketing personnel, and documentation specialists.

○ Make arrangements for the use of work areas for the day of the usability test. Make sure they'll be properly equipped, not only with the relevant computer and software but also with adequate lighting and desktop or table space.

○ Prepare copies of the documentation that include a table of contents and, if at all possible, an index.

Prepare a sheet of instructions for each observer.

USABILITY TEST

Observer's Instructions

You need a copy of the documentation, the volunteer's instruction pamphlet, a pen or pencil, a blank notepad to record your observations, and either a watch or clock. Meet the volunteer at (the prescribed time and place) and escort him or her to the work area. Try to make the volunteer feel at ease and, of course, express our appreciation. To conduct the usability test, you then follow these steps:

1. Hand out the volunteer's instruction sheet and explain that there are several simple exercises to complete, with a time limit for each one.

2. Explain that the goal of the test is to locate any weak areas in the documentation and that the volunteer is to rely on the documentation alone. (You are not to offer assistance or answer questions.)

3. Give the signal to begin and note the time and name of the first exercise.

4. Observe and note the volunteer's reactions, including such things as how long it takes to complete each exercise, the degree of difficulty the volunteer experiences, and which details cause obvious frustration. Note how easy (or difficult) it is for the volunteer to find information and whether he or she uses the table of contents or the index or simply flips through the pages.

5. Halt the volunteer when the prescribed time for each exercise has passed and it's time to begin the next one.

6. When the usability test is over, thank the volunteer again for helping and escort him or her to the front lobby.

After the usability test, compare the results and see which areas consistently caused confusion among the volunteers and which areas caused the greatest degree of frustration. You'll find the test notes very helpful, and you can be sure that the resulting revisions will give your readers better documentation.

GUIDELINES FOR REVISING DRAFTS

Whether you revise your drafts yourself, give them to a typist or word processor, or hand them over to a typesetter or printer, use standard proofreading marks, as shown in Figure 6.1 and Figure 6.2.

Follow these directions for marking revisions:

O Using a colored pencil, write the changes beside the flawed line, in the margin closest to the error.

O When you have two or more corrections in a line, list them from left to right and separate them by slant lines.

O Print substitutions in the margin and then put a caret (^) in the line to mark the place where the substitution should go.

O If you have to delete a character, a word, or words, put a delete mark in the margin and a line through the text that should be deleted.

PROOFREADING MARKS	IN MARGIN	IN TEXT
Insert period	⊙	M.D.
comma	⌃	Wichita,KS
colon	⌃	To:
semicolon	⌃	late;therefore
apostrophe	⌄	don't appear
quotation marks	⌄/ ⌄	"Yes," she said
hyphen	/=/	red-marker area
parentheses	(/)	listed. (See tables.)
dash	1/m	decayed—lead is
ellipsis	#⊙ #⊙ #⊙#	going...factory
space	#	Chapter 2
Paragraph	¶	lessons. ¶ Managers will
No paragraph	No ¶	⌐ The next
Run in on same line	(Run in)	After you finish cutting the panels
Insert here	on/for	Be the alert leakage
Make superscript	⌄2	(x^2)
Make subscript	⌃2	(x_2)
Transpose	(tr)	the of light day
Close up	‿	Ph.D.
Spell out	(sp)	sell 2 or more
Delete	ℓ/ℓ	It is entirely possible
Use lower case	(l.c.)	the last Watch
		the ATLANTIC ocean
Use capital letter	(cap)	detroit, Michigan
Use small capitals	(s.c.)	9:00 a.m.
Set in roman	(Rom)	the filly (Aurora)
Set in italics	(Ital)	the word fire
Set in boldface	(b.f.)	Note: levers
Let it stand (ignore marks)	(stet)	bright and true

Figure 6.1. Proofreading Marks.

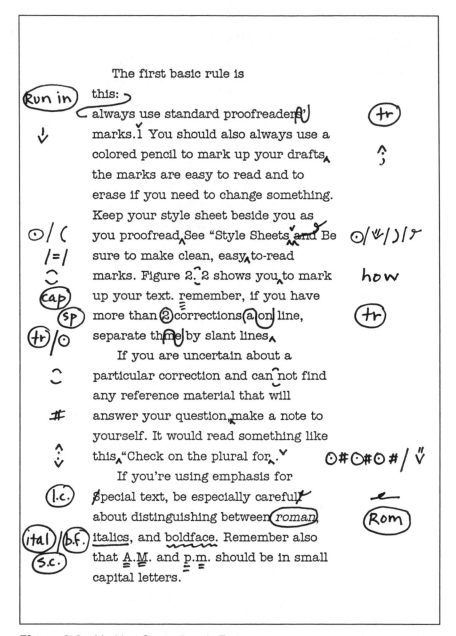

Figure 6.2. Marking Corrections in Text.

REVISING A FIRST DRAFT

1. Use your headings to make an outline. Check the outline to see that you've covered major topics, and then check to see that the subtopics are in place.

2. Using the outline, check to see that your topics and subtopics follow a logical order.

3. Make a first pass through the draft, checking for clarity, flow, and logical order. (It's important to make several passes, concentrating on one thing at a time.) Did you introduce each new topic with a topic statement? Did you put in transitions to lead the readers from topic to topic? Did you arrange your ideas in an order that a reader can easily follow?

4. Read the draft again, but this time be ready to take out every unnecessary word. Get rid of the unnecessary prepositional phrases, the redundancies, the ponderous and pompous words. Be merciless.

5. If your word processing software has a style checker, use it.

6. Now, go through the draft again with your style guide in front of you. Is spelling correct and consistent? Have you used that one term you decided on instead of the two or three that could confuse the reader? Are you following the punctuation, capitalization, and numbers usage defined in the style guide?

7. If your word processing software has a spell checker, use it.

REVISING SUBSEQUENT DRAFTS

1. If you've had a review, use the master copy to incorporate the corrections into your document.

2. Be sure all corrections have been made, that they're in the right location, and that no text before or after has been lost.

3. If you have made major revisions, revise your outline and check to see that topics and subtopics are in place.

4. If you've changed headings or titles for chapters or sections, make sure you have changed any references to them in other parts of the document.

5. Read through the revised portions of the document, checking it against your style guide for inconsistencies.

6. If you're using word processing software that includes a spell checker, use it to correct any misspellings.

7. Check any completed illustrations, including the text of callouts and titles, to make sure they are correct.

PREPARING THE FINAL DRAFT

1. Repeat the steps in the previous section, "Revising Subsequent Drafts."

2. When the illustrations are in place, make sure they are positioned correctly.

3. Be sure the page numbers are in order. (It's surprising how often pages are omitted or duplicated.)

4. Make sure the table of contents lists the correct headings and page numbers.

5. Check all the cross-references.

6. If you have a list of figures or tables, make sure that it lists the correct page numbers.

7. Check the titles in your list of figures and tables against the titles in the text.

8. If you have an index, do a spot check to make sure the page numbers are correct. Check the first five entries and then every fifth one.

9. If you're using word processing software that has a spell checker, use it.

Now your document is as perfect as you can make it, it's ready for publication.

CHAPTER 7

Corrections,
Addenda, and
New Versions

No computer program remains static for long, and trying to document the software is often like trying to zero in on a moving target. It's the nature of the business. Sooner or later, you have to make changes and additions to the documentation because the software has been altered.

Changes to documentation fall into these categories:

TYPE	CAUSES
Correction	Incorrect information was printed
Addendum	Something was added to the software after the documentation was printed, information was omitted from the documentation, or changes were made to the software since the last version.

TYPE	*CAUSES*
New version	Many changes were made to the software, requiring a complete revision and reprinting of the documentation

HANDLING CORRECTIONS

If you need to correct an existing manual, you can do it in one of three ways:

○ Print replacement pages (when the manual is in a ring binder or brad-type binding).

○ Print additional pages for the front of the manual (again, when the binding permits).

○ Include a README file on a software disk that will accompany the manual, and be sure to alert users to its presence.

PRINTING REPLACEMENT PAGES

If you have access to the printed manuals, and if they are in ring binders or brad-type binders where pages can be easily inserted and removed, you can simply print new pages to replace incorrect pages in the manuals. If the manuals are already in the hands of the users, then you must send them the new pages so they can replace the pages. When mailing replacement pages, be sure to include a separate instruction page that briefly states why the re-placement pages are included and what to do with them.

Use the existing page numbers. In other words, replace page 3-13 with page 3-13, but be sure to label the new pages as revisions so the users can't mix up old and new pages.

For example, the running head on a replacement page might read "Revised—11/13/89—Page 3-13." When corrected pages outnumber the old pages, add letters to page numbers on the replacement pages. For example, to add two new pages between pages 3-13 and 3-14, number the new pages 3-13a and 3-13b.

PRINTING ADDITIONAL PAGES

A simpler alternative to replacing pages is to print a list of corrections to insert in the front of the manual. Label the new pages clearly (you might use a running head that says "Corrections to *Manual Name*—11/13/89—Page 01"). List the corrections by page number and heading, like this:

Page 39, "Interrupting a Routine." The procedure should say:
To interrupt a routine that is executing:
    Press Ctrl + Break.

Page 72, "Writing to a File." Step 3 should say:
3. After the program informs you that all information has been written to the file, type *CLOSE FILE* at the prompt and press Enter.

Page 115, "Searching Strings." The NOTE at the top of the page should say:
NOTE: In version 3.0, you can use the /u or /l switches to confine a search to uppercase or lowercase text. In earlier versions, you must type the precise text you want to match.

USING README FILES

Sometimes you might want to list corrections in a file on one of the software disks. Many users are familiar with these types of "add-on" files, which are commonly named

README to encourage the users to do just that. If you decide to use a README file instead of printing corrections, be sure to

○ alert users to the file's presence

○ tell users how to view the information in the file

One method of telling users about a README file is to include a page of instructions with the documentation. If the software includes an installation program, you have the choice of an additional method. Add a module to the installation program that not only informs readers about the README file but also provides the means to display it. For example, such a module might look like this:

THE PROGRAM IS NOW INSTALLED. TO START THE PROGRAM, TYPE *ABC* AT THE SYSTEM PROMPT.

THE LATEST ADDITIONS AND CORRECTIONS TO THIS PROGRAM ARE CONTAINED IN A FILE NAMED *README* ON THE PROGRAM DISK. YOU CAN PRINT THIS FILE BY TYPING *PRINT A:README* AT THE PROMPT.

WOULD YOU LIKE TO VIEW THE README FILE NOW? (PRESS *Y* OR *N*.)

HANDLING ADDENDA

If you inadvertently omit a section from the manual or if something new has been added since the documentation was printed, you can issue an addendum. If the information is not lengthy, your addendum may consist of only a few pages, which users will insert into the front of the manual. If the information is more substantive, the addendum may be a separate, small booklet.

There are two guidelines for handling addenda:

○ Include an introductory page or paragraph explaining why this new material has been issued and exactly what is included in the new material (*n* pages, this booklet, *n* disks labeled *xxx* and *xxx*).

○ Make sure the addendum matches the style and layout of the manual it supplements.

HANDLING NEW VERSIONS

Creating a new version of a software program and its accompanying documentation can be a whole new project, especially if the software has changed radically. You have to begin again at the planning stage and map out a new schedule. However, you do have the advantage of working with an existing manual, which you can use to map out changes and additions.

Once you have a list of software additions and revisions, creating a new version of the documentation is much like handling the corrections after a first review. You write the new sections, revise the old ones, and make sure all the transitions and cross-references get updated as necessary. It's also a good idea to include an introductory section that explains how this new version of the software differs from the previous version. So users won't be confused, be sure to clearly label the software disks and the documentation with the version number.

PART TWO

ORGANIZING SOFTWARE DOC- UMENTATION

Tutorials, procedures guides, reference materials, quick reference pieces, and on-line help systems—each type of software documentation has a different goal.

This part of the book describes each type and tells you how to decide which ones you need and how to organize them. It also gives you examples of each type, excerpted from existing software documentation, so you can see what goes into each type and what makes it successful.

CHAPTER 8

Types of Documentation

Software documentation falls into five basic categories:

CATEGORY	DESCRIPTION
Tutorial	Teaches basic program functions through controlled "hands-on" practice sessions
Procedures guide	Explains and gives step-by-step instructions about how to perform all the functions of the program
Reference material	Describes in detail commands, functions, fields, key assignments, and/or messages
Quick reference piece	Lists the most frequently used commands, functions, or key assignments (may be a card, keyboard template, or small guide booklet)

CATEGORY	DESCRIPTION
On-line help system	Displays information on the screen while the program is running

You'll find out more about how to structure the different types of documentation in Chapters 10 through 14.

WHICH TYPES OF DOCUMENTATION DO YOU NEED?

Which types of documentation do you need? Do you need only a procedures guide? Do you need a complete package that includes every type of documentation? That depends on the needs of your audience. The following chart can help you decide:

TYPE	USE WHEN	ADVANTAGES
Tutorial	Users are novices	Builds confidence
	Users must teach themselves	Lets users practice
	Users need to get started quickly	Allows quick, user-friendly use of program features
	Program is complex or interface is intimidating	

TYPE	USE WHEN	ADVANTAGES
Procedures guide	Users have some experience or program is simple	Allows users to choose only procedures they need
		Information is complete, arranged in task-oriented groupings
Reference material	Users know how to use features and are familiar with interface	Allows quick access to details
		Allows users to approach information from many angles
Quick reference piece	Users are experienced with program	Quickly reminds users which commands, functions, or keys to use
On-line help system	Users need information while running the program	Allows users to get assistance without looking away from the screen

Your decision about which types of documentation to produce depends on the needs of your users and on your budget and schedule. If you're documenting an application, you may be able to get by with only a procedures guide. If you're documenting a programming language, you might want to write only a reference manual.

Generally speaking, no one type of documentation can please all types of users. And there's an additional "growth" problem with documentation: novice users quickly become intermediate users, who then become experienced users, so what pleases your readers in the beginning may not always please them six months down the road. For this reason, the more types of documentation you can include with the software, the better you'll be able to "sell" the program to the users, whether the software is for in-house use or for a retail package.

ONE MANUAL, OR MORE?

Just because we say there are several categories of documentation doesn't mean that each category has to be a separate manual. If your documentation has to serve a wide variety of users but your budget is limited, you may want to combine several types of documentation to create a combination manual, which you would organize as follows:

Part I: Tutorial

Part II: Procedures Guide

Part III: Reference Materials

Users can then skip to the part of the manual they need. To provide users with quick reference pieces, you could add a perforated quick reference card that users can tear out of the manual, print quick reference information inside the front cover or on the back cover, or just list that information on a separate page for easy access.

Keep in mind, though, that huge manuals are intimidating to users and can make the program seem complicated and unfriendly. So if you find that a combination manual exceeds 400 pages, it's a good idea to consider dividing the information into two or more manuals.

If you decide to use more than one manual, you'll need to duplicate some information, because you can't assume that users will memorize (or even be aware of) the information in the other manuals. For example, each manual in a set needs

- an overview of how the manual fits into the package (i.e., one of a five-part set) and what each manual or piece contains

- a table of contents

- an explanation of conventions used in the manual

- definitions of terms

- an index

In the following chapters, you'll find out what each type of documentation contains, learn how to organize each type of documentation, and see examples from existing manuals and on-line documentation.

CHAPTER 9

The Parts of a Document

Documents are usually made up of three major sections: the front matter, the main text, and the back matter. The contents of the main text in each type of document discussed in Chapter 8 will vary. However, the front matter and the back matter in most documents contain similar parts, as illustrated in Figure 9.1.

Front matter contains some or all of the following parts:

○ title page

○ copyright or acknowledgments page

○ table of contents

○ list of figures and/or tables

○ symbols and conventions page

○ installation and start-up guidelines

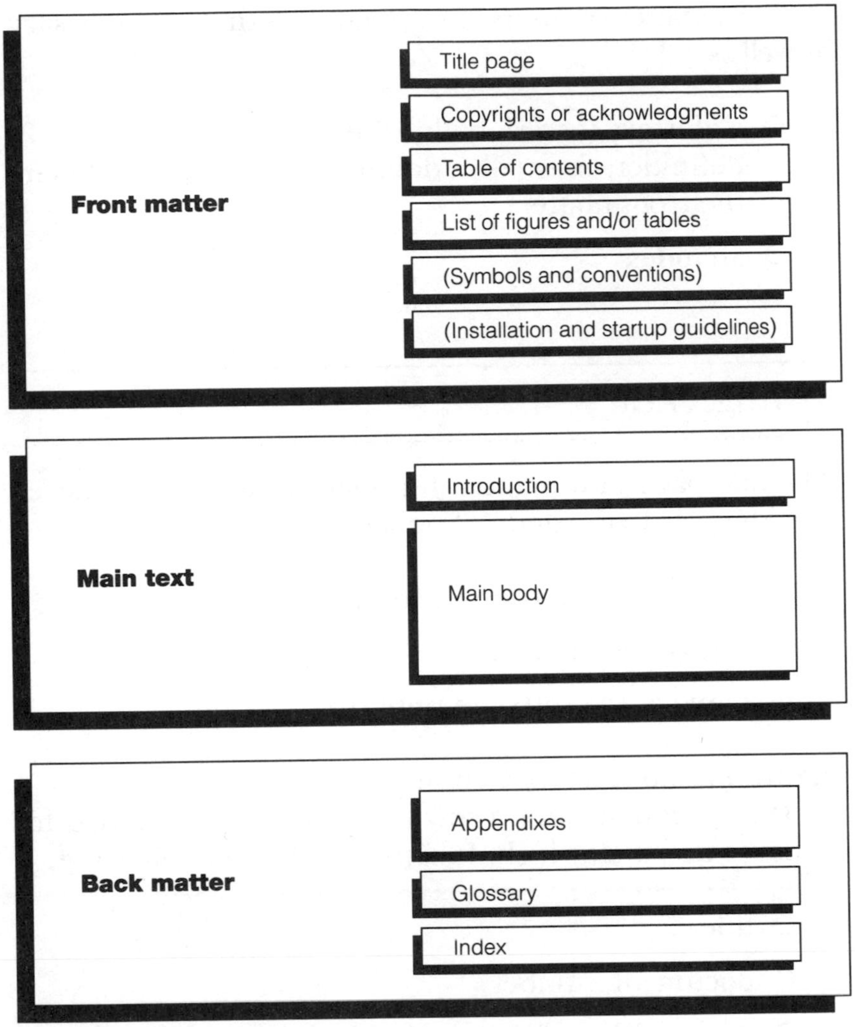

Front matter
- Title page
- Copyrights or acknowledgments
- Table of contents
- List of figures and/or tables
- (Symbols and conventions)
- (Installation and startup guidelines)

Main text
- Introduction
- Main body

Back matter
- Appendixes
- Glossary
- Index

Figure 9.1. Parts of a Document. Parts enclosed in parentheses are sometimes included elsewhere. Symbols and conventions may often be found in the introduction. Installation and start-up information may be found in the introduction, in an appendix, or sometimes in a separate booklet.

Back matter contains any appendixes that are necessary, as well as

○ a glossary (occasionally, when the number of definitions is small, a definitions page is included in the front matter)

○ an index

TITLE PAGE

The title page of a manual for a software program developed for sale to the general public may include

○ name of the software program

○ title of the manual

○ name of the software publisher

Figure 9.2 shows a typical title page.

If the manual is for a software program developed for in-house use, it may include some or all of the following:

○ title

○ document number

○ name of the author and/or the editor

○ name of the department issuing the document and the supervisor

○ date of issue

○ security classifications

Figure 9.2. Title Page (from *Learning Aldus FreeHand*).

COPYRIGHT OR ACKNOWLEDGMENTS PAGE

When you include material in your document (text or art) from another source, that material may be copyrighted. If so, you need to get permission to use it. The company that owns the material may require you to use their prescribed credit line or let you use a standard credit line of your own creation. In addition, you should acknowledge the trademarks of any companies and products you mention in your document. The major elements on a copyright page are

○ copyright information for the document

○ trademark information for your product and any others mentioned in the document

In addition, a copyright page may include

○ production credits

○ licensing information

○ revision and edition information

○ warranties and disclaimers

○ telephone number for support service

○ date

○ manual number

Figures 9.3 and 9.4 show typical copyright pages.

COPYRIGHT NOTICE

No part of this publication may be reproduced, transmitted, transcribed, stored in a retrieval system, or translated into any human or computer language, in any form or by any means, without the express written permission of Traveling Software, Inc.

TRADEMARKS

Traveling Software and the Traveling Software suitcase logo are registered trademarks of Traveling Software, Inc.

Wizard PC-Link is a trademark of Traveling Software, Inc.

IBM is a registered trademark of International Business Machines Corporation.
Lotus and 1-2-3 are registered trademarks of Lotus Corporation.
Sidekick is a trademark of Borland International, Inc..
dBASE is a trademark of Ashton-Tate.
R:Base is a trademark of Microrim.
Excel is a trademark of Microsoft Corporation.

For technical support, call: (206) 483-8088

Wizard PC-Link
© 1988, 1989 Traveling Software, Inc. All rights reserved.
18702 North Creek Parkway
Bothell, WA 98011
U. S. A.
(206) 483-8088

Wizard PC-Link Manual
© 1989 by Traveling Software, Inc.

May 1989

ii

Figure 9.3. Copyright Page (from *Wizard PC-Link Manual*).

II User's Manual

CREDITS

Concept and Direction	Wayne Erickson, Fred Gray, Marco Hegyi, David Hull
Documentation	Laurel Check, Marva Dasef, Kerri Mathis, Dan Monda
Product Control	Kim Asay, J. Keith Bankston, Trish Hall, Kay Lawson
Product Marketing	Penny Grote, Bill White
Operations	Cliff Hewitt
Programming and Design	John Lette, Colin Miller, Dean Tally
Technical Support	Steve Alboucq
Corporate Dedication to Quality	All employees at Microrim

COPYRIGHT

COPYRIGHT © by Microrim, Inc., 1987. All rights reserved. No part of this publication may be reproduced, transmitted, transcribed, stored in a retrieval system, or translated into any language in any format by any means, without the written permission of Microrim, Inc.

TRADEMARKS

Microrim and R:BASE are registered trademarks of Microrim, Inc.
DB Graphics is a trademark of Microrim, Inc.
dBASE, dBASE III, dBASE III Plus, and Ashton-Tate are registered trademarks of Ashton-Tate.

IBM, PC, AT, XT, PC Convertible, and Personal System/2 are trademarks of International Business Machines Corporation.
GSS is a registered trademark of Graphic Software Systems, Inc.
Hercules is a trademark of Hercules Computer Technology, Inc.

SOFTWARE COPYRIGHT NOTICE

Your license agreement with Microrim, Inc., authorizes the number of copies which can be made and the computer system(s) on which they may be used. Any unauthorized duplication or use of DB Graphics in whole or in part, in print or in any other storage-and-retrieval system, is forbidden.

The GSSCGI.SYS program and GSS device drivers are proprietary products of Graphic Software Systems, Inc., Beaverton, Oregon.

DISCLAIMER

Names and references to persons, corporations, or products that are used in the examples of this manual are intentionally fictional. Any resemblance to persons living or dead or to actual corporations or products is purely coincidental.

First Edition
DB Graphics
User's Manual
UD4090-00
Version 1.0
September, 1987

Figure 9.4. Copyright Page (from *DB Graphics User's Manual*).

TABLE OF CONTENTS

A table of contents usually includes all of the headings in the manual. Figures 9.5, 9.6, and 9.7 show excerpts from some typical tables of contents.

LIST OF FIGURES AND/OR TABLES

For your readers' convenience, you may decide to list the figures and tables in the front matter, as shown in Figure 9.8.

CONTENTS

CONTENTS

Figure 9.5. Table of Contents (from Bedford's *Integrated Accounting User's Guide*).

Table of Contents

v

Introduction

Figure 9.6. Table of Contents for a Manual with Numbered Sections (from *Microsoft QuickBASIC: Programming in BASIC*).

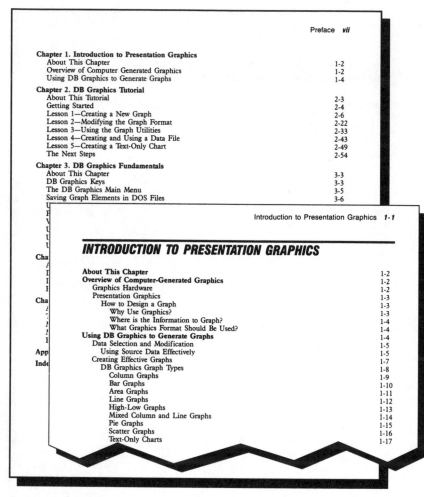

Figure 9.7. Tables of Contents (from *DB Graphics User's Manual*). This document's table of contents lists only major headings, and a more detailed chapter outline introduces each chapter.

Figures

xviii

Figure 9.8. List of Figures (from *Microsoft QuickBASIC: Programming in BASIC*).

SYMBOLS AND CONVENTIONS PAGE

You can include a section in the introduction that describes the symbols and conventions used in the manual, or you can devote a page in the front matter to this information. Figures 9.9 and 9.10 illustrate.

Typographical conventions

In this manual, the ☞ callout emphasizes important points.

When a specialized term is used for the first time, it appears in boldface. Chapter names mentioned in the text also appear in bold, as do the names of menu, mode, and keyboard commands when they refer to actions which you should perform. Names of computer files and directories appear in upper case boldface.

Throughout this manual, when you see **Enter** you should press the **Enter** key (sometimes called the **Return** key.)

The term **Mouse Cursor** refers to the cursor that moves when you move the mouse. The shape of this cursor depends on the function selected, (see Figure 3–2) and on the nature of the action being performed.

The term **Text Cursor** refers to the vertical line cursor that indicates the location where text is currently being added or deleted. The text cursor is always placed **between** characters, and is active only when you are operating in **Text** mode.

Throughout this manual, the phrase **Select the...** is used. This means you should move the mouse cursor to the middle of the item that you are going to select, and then press the left mouse button once.

Except when explicitly stated otherwise, the computer hard disk is always assumed to be **C**. The term **Floppy Disk** refers to either $5\frac{1}{4}$" or $3\frac{1}{2}$" diskettes.

Figure 9.9. Symbols and Conventions (from *Xerox Ventura Publisher Reference Guide*).

Notational Conventions

This manual uses the following notation:

Example of Convention	Description of Convention
Example	The typeface shown in the left column is used to simulate the appearance of information that would be printed on the screen or by the printer.
placeholders	Words in italics are placeholders in command-line and option specifications for types of information that you must supply. Italics are also occasionally used in the text for emphasis.

xxiv

Figure 9.10.   Symbols and Conventions (from *Microsoft QuickC Programmer's Guide*).

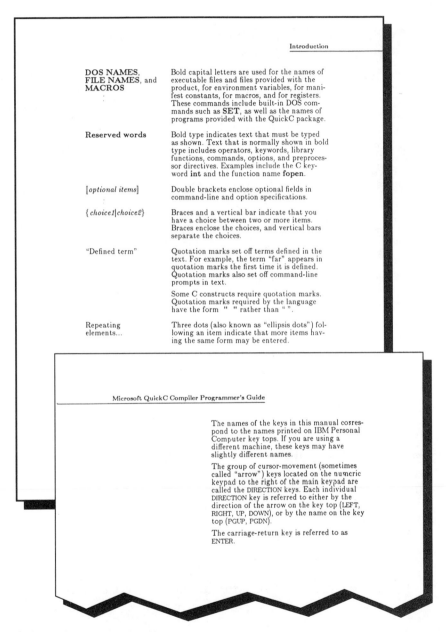

DOS NAMES, FILE NAMES, and **MACROS**	Bold capital letters are used for the names of executable files and files provided with the product, for environment variables, for manifest constants, for macros, and for registers. These commands include built-in DOS commands such as **SET**, as well as the names of programs provided with the QuickC package.
Reserved words	Bold type indicates text that must be typed as shown. Text that is normally shown in bold type includes operators, keywords, library functions, commands, options, and preprocessor directives. Examples include the C keyword **int** and the function name **fopen**.
[*optional items*]	Double brackets enclose optional fields in command-line and option specifications.
{*choice1*|*choice2*}	Braces and a vertical bar indicate that you have a choice between two or more items. Braces enclose the choices, and vertical bars separate the choices.
"Defined term"	Quotation marks set off terms defined in the text. For example, the term "far" appears in quotation marks the first time it is defined. Quotation marks also set off command-line prompts in text.
	Some C constructs require quotation marks. Quotation marks required by the language have the form " " rather than " ".
Repeating elements...	Three dots (also known as "ellipsis dots") following an item indicate that more items having the same form may be entered.

Microsoft QuickC Compiler Programmer's Guide

The names of the keys in this manual correspond to the names printed on IBM Personal Computer key tops. If you are using a different machine, these keys may have slightly different names.

The group of cursor-movement (sometimes called "arrow") keys located on the numeric keypad to the right of the main keypad are called the DIRECTION keys. Each individual DIRECTION key is referred to either by the direction of the arrow on the key top (LEFT, RIGHT, UP, DOWN), or by the name on the key top (PGUP, PGDN).

The carriage-return key is referred to as ENTER.

Figure 9.10 (continued).

INSTALLATION AND START-UP GUIDELINES

Most documentation includes information on installing and starting the program. Some packages include a "SETUP" installation program on one of the disks. But even if most of the process is automated, you must include written instructions that tell users how to find the SETUP file and how to start the process.

You can place installation and start-up information

- on the outside cover
- in a separate pamphlet
- in the front matter
- in the introduction
- in an appendix

Start-up and installation information includes some or all of the following:

- hardware requirements
- system requirements
- contents of the disk(s)
- how to install the program
- how to get out of trouble
- how to start and quit the program
- a description of the interface, how to use menus, or how to enter or select commands
- how to use the manual

For instance, here is an outline of the information in an appendix to the manual for *who·what·when*, a people, project, and time management program:

```
System Requirements
Directory
Installation
Filling Out the Primary User Screen
Keys
Configuring Your System
   The Path
   CONFIG.SYS
   Starting Automatically
   Memory Resident Alarm
Troubleshooting
   Screen Is Hard to Read
   Blank Screen
   Program Does Not Run
   Program Runs Slowly
   Using a Local Area Network
```

Figure 9.11 is an example of start-up information included in a manual's introduction.

GLOSSARY

When you introduce a lot of terms that readers may not be familiar with, you need a glossary (often titled "Terms"). You'll also define each new term in the text the first time you mention it, of course. In some in-house manuals, the company may use a format that includes a "Definition of Terms" page in the front matter instead of a glossary.

Figure 9.12 shows an excerpt from a glossary.

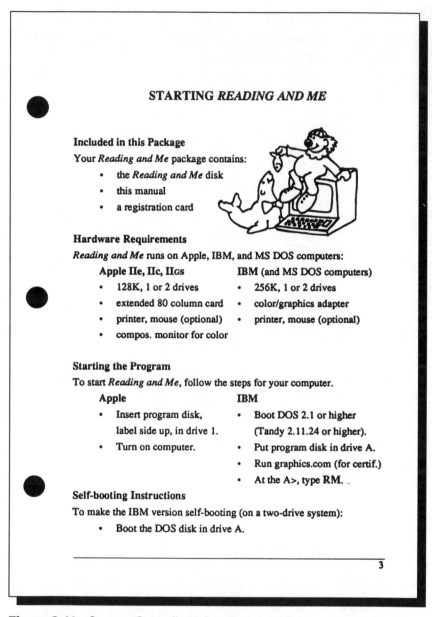

STARTING *READING AND ME*

Included in this Package

Your *Reading and Me* package contains:

- the *Reading and Me* disk
- this manual
- a registration card

Hardware Requirements

Reading and Me runs on Apple, IBM, and MS DOS computers:

Apple IIe, IIc, IIGS

- 128K, 1 or 2 drives
- extended 80 column card
- printer, mouse (optional)
- compos. monitor for color

IBM (and MS DOS computers)

- 256K, 1 or 2 drives
- color/graphics adapter
- printer, mouse (optional)

Starting the Program

To start *Reading and Me*, follow the steps for your computer.

Apple

- Insert program disk, label side up, in drive 1.
- Turn on computer.

IBM

- Boot DOS 2.1 or higher (Tandy 2.11.24 or higher).
- Put program disk in drive A.
- Run graphics.com (for certif.)
- At the A>, type RM. ...

Self-booting Instructions

To make the IBM version self-booting (on a two-drive system):

- Boot the DOS disk in drive A.

3

Figure 9.11. Start-up Guide (from *Reading and Me*).

- Insert the *Reading and Me* program disk in drive B.
- Type **sys b: <Return>**. Follow the screen prompts. (For one drive, insert the program disk when prompted for the disk for drive B; insert DOS when prompted for the disk for drive A.)
- At the next A>, type **copy command.com b: <Return>**.
- At the next A>, type **copy graphics.com b: <Return>**.

(If you wish to copy the program to a hard disk, see Appendix C.)

Signing In

On the opening screen, you will see a dialog box.

- Have your child enter his name in the dialog box **<Return>**.

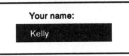

Registering Your Five-year Warranty

Davidson & Associates, Inc. provides a five-year warranty on *Reading and Me* and will replace, free of charge, any damaged or malfunctioning disk. Complete and return the enclosed registration card. This ensures that you will receive information about the latest updates and new programs.

Purchasing a Back-up Copy

Program files are copy-protected. You may purchase a back-up for $10.00 (3.5" or 5.25"). Back-ups are not available for lab packs.

4

Figure 9.11 (continued).

Glossary   E

access	to connect successfully to another computer.
alternate program	a program, macro, or batch file that you set up to run from the First Choice Main Menu.
applications	different tools you use to accomplish various tasks. With First Choice, you have word processing, database management, spreadsheet analysis, graphics, and electronic communications.
ASCII	the letters ASCII (pronounced ASK-key) stand for the American Standard Code for Information Interchange. An ASCII file is a disk file containing characters in ASCII code.
cell	where a row and column intersect in a spreadsheet. A cell is referenced by the row and column it is in—R1C1 for example—or by its name.
character	a letter, number, space, punctuation mark, or any other symbol you can type from the keyboard.
communication	the process of passing information and commands from one computer to another.
communications settings	the term First Choice uses for settings such as modem speed, number of stop bits, and parity, which affect the way information is sent and received. Your computer, all equipment along the path to the service, and the remote computer must use the same communications settings.
connect time	the clock time that has elapsed since you signed on to a service (for which you may be charged).
cursor	the symbol on the screen that shows you where you are and where the next action will occur.
database	a collection of records that are of the same type. First Choice keeps a form design you create, along with all the records, in a database.
data directory	a subdivision on a hard disk where data files created with an application are stored.
default	the value the program sets automatically whenever several values can be chosen.

Glossary   E-1

Figure 9.12. Glossary (from *PFS: First Choice*® *Version 3.02*).

INDEX

Readers are always grateful when they find a carefully pre-pared index. Here are some guidelines:

○ Put yourself in the readers' place and try to foresee which details they'll try to locate in the index.

○ Don't duplicate the table of contents.

○ Include synonyms for terms that may not be meaningful to readers. For instance, if your command for loading files in your word processing program is "Transfer Load," you might include entries under "Loading files," "Opening files," and "Files, loading" as well. If your readers are novices, you might also include "Starting new files," or "Starting new documents."

○ Use two or three levels of entries unless your document is short or the subject matter simple, in which case you can use one level.

○ Include 1 to 4 pages of index entries for every 100 pages in your manual, depending on the complexity of the information.

Figures 9.13, 9.14, and 9.15 show examples of indexes.

I-12 User's Manual

Figure 9.13. Combination Index and Glossary (from *DB Graphics User's Manual*).

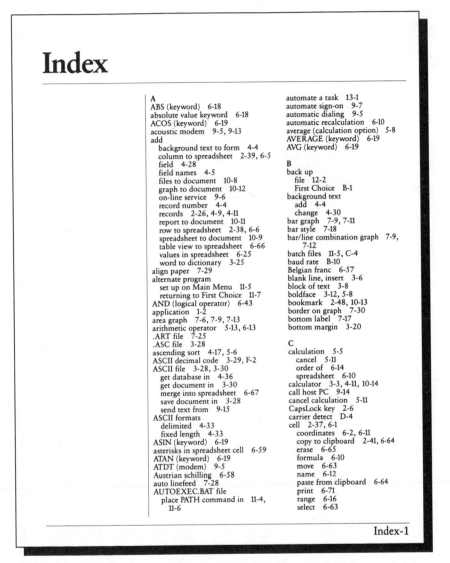

Index

Figure 9.14. Index (from *PFS: First Choice® Version 3.02*). This page is from a fourteen-page index for a moderately long manual.

Index

Archive attribute - 26, 33
Attributes, file - 25, 33
Audio feedback - 30
AUTOEXEC.BAT file - 5

Baud rate - 1, 11, 33
Batch operation - 31, 35
Beep - 30

Cable - 5, C-1
COM1, COM2 - 5, 11
Command line operation - 31, 33, 34
Command to start program - 7, 31
Connectors, cable - 5, C-1
Communications lost - 12, 16, A-4
CONFIG.SYS file - 5
Copying program files - 6
Copy protection - 1, 16
Copyright notice - Inside cover
Create directory - 18
Current directory - 8, 17, 29, 33
Cursor movement - 10
Customizing - 29

Delete directory - 27
Delete file - 21
Directory - 8, 14, 17, 19, 29, 33
Directory tree - 19
Display area - 8
DOS commands - 27, 31

Enter key - 7
Epson Equity - 11
Error messages - A-1
Escape key - 9
Exiting - 4, 28, 29, 33

File names - 19, 20, 23, 29

(continued...)

Index-1

Figure 9.15. Index (from *Rapid Relay User Manual*). This page is from a 2½ page index for a short manual.

CHAPTER 10

Organizing Tutorials

A tutorial consists of one or more controlled "hands-on" practice sessions that teach users how to perform the basic functions of your program. A tutorial has two goals: to build confidence in novice users and to enable them to use the program quickly.

Every tutorial should include

○ an overview of how to use the program

○ explanations of basic concepts and definitions of new terms

○ step-by-step procedures that tell users exactly what to type, which options to choose, which key to press, and so forth

A tutorial should help users feel comfortable with the program's interface, so it should show them how to

○ start the program

○ choose or enter a command or function, fill in a field, or specify an option (whatever is required to get basic work done)

○ get help (if there's an on-line help system)

○ cancel if something goes wrong

○ exit from the program

A good tutorial then leads the readers through the basics of using the program. For example, an outline for a tutorial about a charting program might look like this:

I. OVERVIEW
Description of what the program does
Basic steps in using the program

II. LEARNING THE BASICS (lesson modules)
Start the program
Choose a command (to load a supplied file)
Choose options for that command
Carry out the command
Choose another command
Get help about that command
Cancel the command
Exit from the program

III. CREATING A CHART (lesson modules)
Enter the data
Choose a chart type
Display the chart
Improve the chart
Save the file
Exit from the program

GENERAL GUIDELINES FOR TUTORIALS

To write an effective tutorial, follow these guidelines:

- ○ Keep modules short. If new users cannot quickly see results, they become frustrated and bored. For example, never ask users to type more than a few lines of text.

- ○ Make sure instructions aren't repetitious. Don't repeat a sequence of actions any more than is necessary to get your point across. Although it may seem logical to enter fifty records in a data base, don't ask your users to type more than three or four. They'll get the idea.

- ○ Write *complete* instructions. Describe the results of the users' actions where appropriate. Reassure users when they see a display that might alarm or confuse them. Also, mention any messages that may appear during the process. To show step-by-step progress, include illustrations or screen shots.

To control the environment and keep the instructions short, you might have users begin with a file that you've set up for them. For example, if you're teaching how to write a BASIC sorting routine, you could provide the data files to sort. This would let users concentrate on learning how to write the sorting routine, not on entering a lot of data.

CHOOSING A SCENARIO

To make your tutorial more interesting, motivate users, and give them a feeling of accomplishment, include a scenario. A *scenario* for a tutorial can be defined as a "plot" or a projected sequence of events. You set up a scenario just as you would sketch out the plot of a screenplay: you describe the current situation, then you set a goal, and then you move the action toward that goal.

A scenario can be set up with as little as one or two sentences and—if appropriate—a graphic. For example, if you were writing a tutorial for a graphics presentation program, you might start off with something like this:

> The boss has assigned you the task of presenting the annual
> sales summary at the company meeting. You've decided that
> your presentation should begin with a slide that looks like this:
>   [PRESENTATION SLIDE HERE]

For a scheduling program, your scenario might begin in this way:

> Your company has won the contract to build the new high
> school auditorium, and now you've got to project your schedule.

You might even want to invent a fictitious company name and a few fictitious characters to make the scenario more interesting. Adding a splash of humor and imagination can make learning easier, as long as you don't cross over the line into ridiculous situations or use insulting language. Here are two basic guidelines for creating a scenario:

○ Choose a goal that your users can relate to—an end result that they might really want to accomplish in their daily work.

○ Plan a result that showcases the easily mastered capabilities of your program. A good scenario should show off the power of the program, but each module should take no longer than one hour for users to work through.

When you've set up your scenario, the next step is to lead users through the steps necessary to reach the goal you've described.

ON-LINE TUTORIALS VS. PRINTED TUTORIALS

Printed tutorials have been around for decades, usually in the form of workbooks and classroom lessons. On-line tutorials have become very popular in recent years. Here's a comparison of the two types:

TYPE	ADVANTAGES	DISADVANTAGES
On-line	Allows users to practice with the program (or a simulation of the program) in a controlled environment	Frequently requires programming ability and special software
	Gives immediate responses to actions (assuming adequate response analysis is built in)	Can be expensive and technically difficult to produce
	Because it's on the monitor screen, is usually flashier than a printed tutorial	Can eat up a great deal of disk space and memory

TYPE	ADVANTAGES	DISADVANTAGES
Printed	Does not occupy computer memory or disk space	Is not as flashy as an on-line tutorial
	Because users can read more words on paper than on a computer screen, can cover more ground than an on-line tutorial	Requires users to switch attention back and forth between the monitor screen and the tutorial pages
	Is reasonably cheap and easy to produce	Offers no immediate response to actions other than those provided by the program itself

BASIC ORGANIZATIONS FOR TUTORIAL MODULES

The overall organization for a tutorial should be a logical, utilitarian sequence that presents information in the order users need it. For example, ask users to enter information before you ask them to edit it, because this would be the normal progression of their work.

The tutorial should be divided into short instructional modules or "lessons." You then use the following basic structure for each tutorial module:

1. any necessary preliminary information (such as descriptions of assumed conditions, definitions of terms, explanations of concepts needed to understand the following procedure, and so forth)

2. statement of goal

3. procedure

4. statement of accomplishment

SAMPLE TUTORIALS

In this section you'll see selections from both a printed tutorial and from an on-line tutorial.

A PRINTED TUTORIAL

Figure 10.1 shows a small section of the *Learning Aldus Freehand* tutorial. The tutorial is a separate manual that contains the following lessons:

> Lesson 1: The Basics
> Lesson 2: Start from Scratch
> Lesson 3: A Closer Look at the Drawing Tools

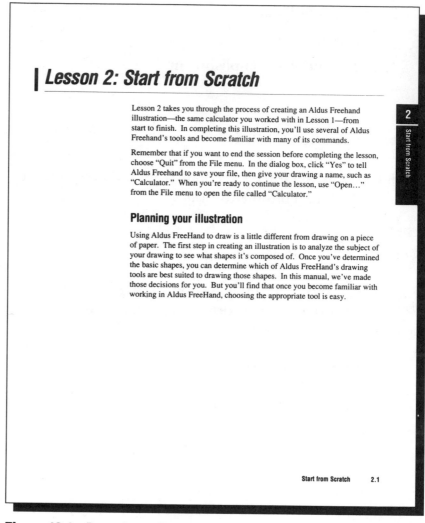

Figure 10.1. Pages from a Tutorial (from *Learning Aldus FreeHand*). Note that the lesson starts with two transitional paragraphs that sum up what was accomplished in the previous lesson and remind users how to interrupt a lesson if necessary. The paragraph under "Planning your illustration" explains that the tutorial has made decisions for users.

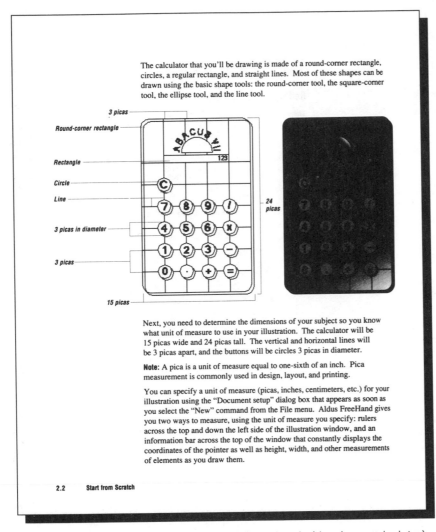

The calculator that you'll be drawing is made of a round-corner rectangle, circles, a regular rectangle, and straight lines. Most of these shapes can be drawn using the basic shape tools: the round-corner tool, the square-corner tool, the ellipse tool, and the line tool.

Next, you need to determine the dimensions of your subject so you know what unit of measure to use in your illustration. The calculator will be 15 picas wide and 24 picas tall. The vertical and horizontal lines will be 3 picas apart, and the buttons will be circles 3 picas in diameter.

Note: A pica is a unit of measure equal to one-sixth of an inch. Pica measurement is commonly used in design, layout, and printing.

You can specify a unit of measure (picas, inches, centimeters, etc.) for your illustration using the "Document setup" dialog box that appears as soon as you select the "New" command from the File menu. Aldus FreeHand gives you two ways to measure, using the unit of measure you specify: rulers across the top and down the left side of the illustration window, and an information bar across the top of the window that constantly displays the coordinates of the pointer as well as height, width, and other measurements of elements as you draw them.

2.2   Start from Scratch

Figure 10.1 (continued). This page sets the scenario (drawing a calculator) and gives definitions and other necessary preliminary information.

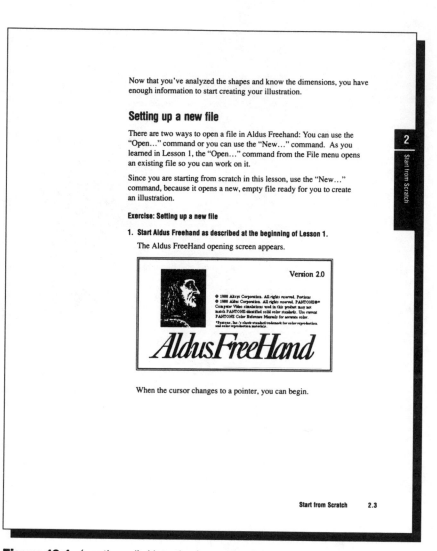

Now that you've analyzed the shapes and know the dimensions, you have enough information to start creating your illustration.

Setting up a new file

There are two ways to open a file in Aldus Freehand: You can use the "Open..." command or you can use the "New..." command. As you learned in Lesson 1, the "Open..." command from the File menu opens an existing file so you can work on it.

Since you are starting from scratch in this lesson, use the "New..." command, because it opens a new, empty file ready for you to create an illustration.

Exercise: Setting up a new file

1. **Start Aldus Freehand as described at the beginning of Lesson 1.**

   The Aldus FreeHand opening screen appears.

When the cursor changes to a pointer, you can begin.

Start from Scratch   2.3

Figure 10.1 (continued). Note the format for the exercise: a section title, "Setting up a new file," followed by an introductory paragraph and an exercise. The exercise is clearly labeled so users will know they're expected to follow the numbered steps.

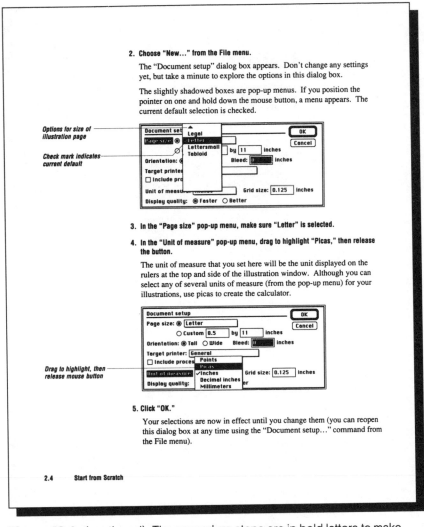

2. Choose "New..." from the File menu.

The "Document setup" dialog box appears. Don't change any settings yet, but take a minute to explore the options in this dialog box.

The slightly shadowed boxes are pop-up menus. If you position the pointer on one and hold down the mouse button, a menu appears. The current default selection is checked.

Options for size of illustration page

Check mark indicates current default

3. In the "Page size" pop-up menu, make sure "Letter" is selected.

4. In the "Unit of measure" pop-up menu, drag to highlight "Picas," then release the button.

The unit of measure that you set here will be the unit displayed on the rulers at the top and side of the illustration window. Although you can select any of several units of measure (from the pop-up menu) for your illustrations, use picas to create the calculator.

Drag to highlight, then release mouse button

5. Click "OK."

Your selections are now in effect until you change them (you can reopen this dialog box at any time using the "Document setup..." command from the File menu).

2.4   Start from Scratch

Figure 10.1 (continued). The procedure steps are in bold letters to make them stand out. Illustrations show users what they'll see on the computer screen.

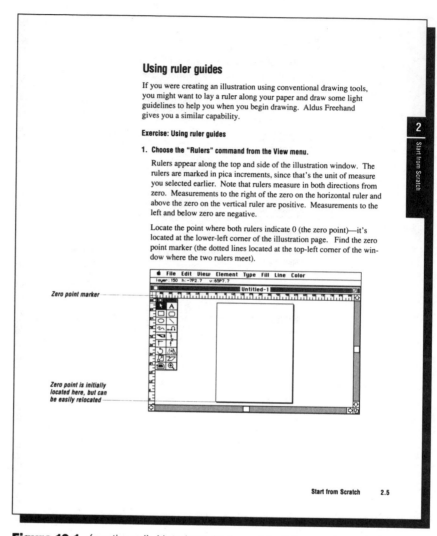

Using ruler guides

If you were creating an illustration using conventional drawing tools, you might want to lay a ruler along your paper and draw some light guidelines to help you when you begin drawing. Aldus Freehand gives you a similar capability.

Exercise: Using ruler guides

1. Choose the "Rulers" command from the View menu.

Rulers appear along the top and side of the illustration window. The rulers are marked in pica increments, since that's the unit of measure you selected earlier. Note that rulers measure in both directions from zero. Measurements to the right of the zero on the horizontal ruler and above the zero on the vertical ruler are positive. Measurements to the left and below zero are negative.

Locate the point where both rulers indicate 0 (the zero point)—it's located at the lower-left corner of the illustration page. Find the zero point marker (the dotted lines located at the top-left corner of the window where the two rulers meet).

Zero point marker

Zero point is initially located here, but can be easily relocated

Start from Scratch   2.5

Figure 10.1 (continued). Note how the format for this exercise matches the previous one. In this manual, the sections are clearly marked both with running feet on all pages and with shaded labels on the outside margins of right-hand pages.

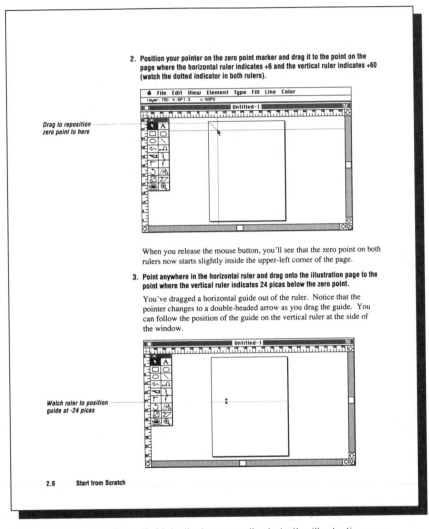

Figure 10.1 (continued). Note that even callouts to the illustrations are instructional.

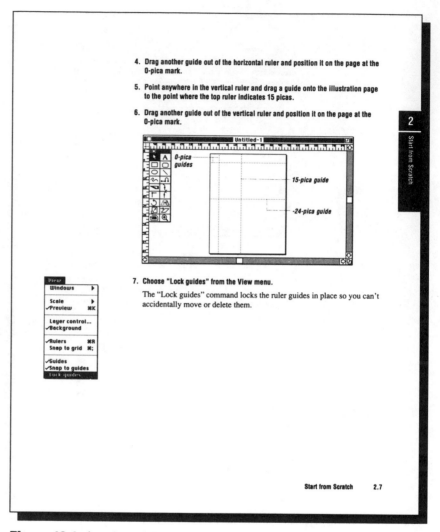

4. Drag another guide out of the horizontal ruler and position it on the page at the 0-pica mark.

5. Point anywhere in the vertical ruler and drag a guide onto the illustration page to the point where the top ruler indicates 15 picas.

6. Drag another guide out of the vertical ruler and position it on the page at the 0-pica mark.

7. Choose "Lock guides" from the View menu.

The "Lock guides" command locks the ruler guides in place so you can't accidentally move or delete them.

Start from Scratch   2.7

Figure 10.1 (continued). The menu graphic at the left side of the page helps users zero in on exactly the command they need.

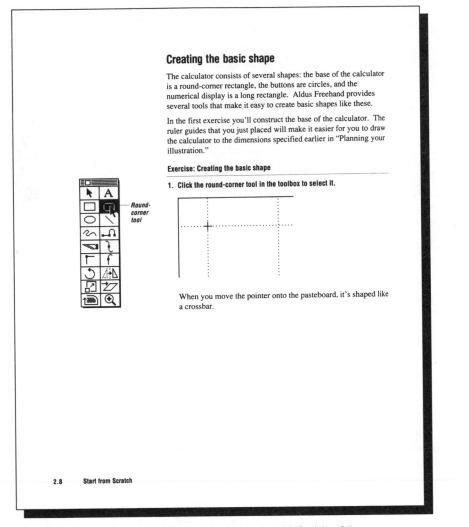

Creating the basic shape

The calculator consists of several shapes: the base of the calculator is a round-corner rectangle, the buttons are circles, and the numerical display is a long rectangle. Aldus Freehand provides several tools that make it easy to create basic shapes like these.

In the first exercise you'll construct the base of the calculator. The ruler guides that you just placed will make it easier for you to draw the calculator to the dimensions specified earlier in "Planning your illustration."

Exercise: Creating the basic shape

1. Click the round-corner tool in the toolbox to select it.

Round-corner tool

When you move the pointer onto the pasteboard, it's shaped like a crossbar.

2.8   Start from Scratch

Figure 10.1 (continued). The tools graphic at the left side of the page shows users where to find tools on the computer screen. This takes the place of a full screen shot.

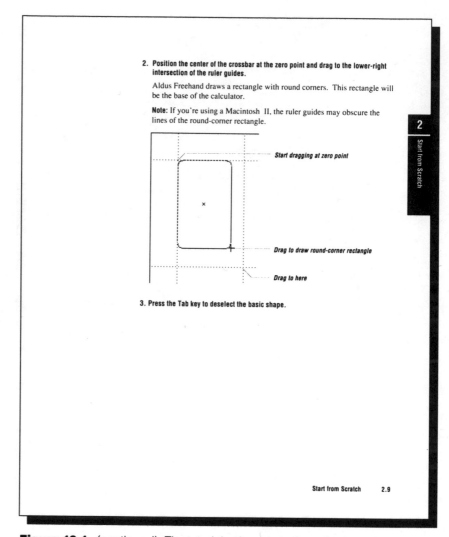

2. Position the center of the crossbar at the zero point and drag to the lower-right intersection of the ruler guides.

Aldus Freehand draws a rectangle with round corners. This rectangle will be the base of the calculator.

Note: If you're using a Macintosh II, the ruler guides may obscure the lines of the round-corner rectangle.

3. Press the Tab key to deselect the basic shape.

Figure 10.1 (continued). The tutorial writer remembered to include a note for special circumstances. This helps Macintosh II users feel secure.

AN ON-LINE TUTORIAL

This section includes a series of screen shots showing a small portion of the *Microsoft® Learning DOS* tutorial (version 2.0). Here's the outline for the complete tutorial:

How to Use This Course
What You Can Accomplish with DOS
Using DOS
  Getting Started
    Starting DOS
    Running an Application
    Viewing Files
    Introducing the DOS 4.0 Shell
  Working with Files
    The Current Drive
    Giving Files Useful Names
    Preparing a Floppy Disk
    Copying Files
    Shortcuts for Copying
    Deleting Files
  Organizing with Directories
    Making a Directory Structure
    Working with Directories
    Removing a Directory
    More Directory Skills
    Using a Directory Tree
  Using Installed Applications
    Setting a Path to Your Tools
    Running Installed Applications
  Backing Up Your Files
    Developing a Backup Procedure
    Backing Up Your Hard Disk
    Backing Up a Floppy Disk
  Advanced Tips
    Mode Settings for Hardware
    Fixed Settings
    Working with Batch Files
    Memory and Storage Devices
Practicing What You've Learned

As you can see, *Learning DOS* is a thorough tutorial: it teaches just about everything a user needs to know about the subject. Figure 10.2 focuses on a small section of the tutorial, the second module of "Shortcuts for Copying," in which users learn to copy and rename a file at the same time.

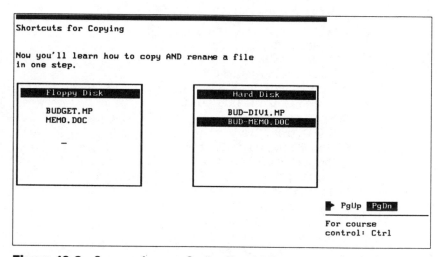

Figure 10.2. Screens from an On-line Tutorial (from *Microsoft Learning DOS*). This screen introduces the tutorial module, stating the basic concept that will be taught.

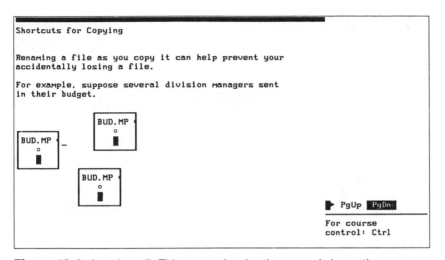

Figure 10.2 (continued). This screen begins the scenario by setting up a hypothetical situation. Note that the title of the lesson module is in the upper left corner of the screen so users know exactly where they are in the course.

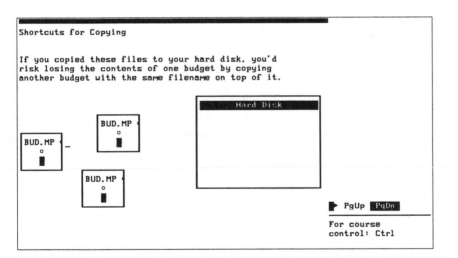

Figure 10.2 (continued). This screen continues the explanation of the scenario. Note the pointer in the lower right corner of the screen. By highlighting **PgDn** and positioning the pointer beside the key names, the screen suggests that users press **PgDn**, which displays the next screen.

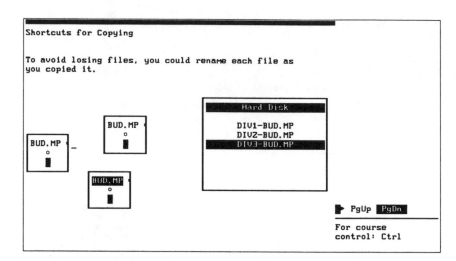

```
Shortcuts for Copying

To avoid losing files, you could rename each file as
you copied it.
```

Figure 10.2 (continued). The scenario continues. In the lower right corner of each screen, you see "For course control: **Ctrl**." This tells users that pressing **Ctrl** will display a menu of commands that allow them to move to different locations in the tutorial.

```
Shortcuts for Copying

To copy and rename a file in one step, you'll include
a new name for the file as part of the target.

        C>copy a:filename.ext c:newname.ext





        _




                                                 ▶ PgUp  PgDn

                                                 For course
                                                 control: Ctrl
```

Figure 10.2 (continued). This screen tells users what they will be doing in the upcoming practice session.

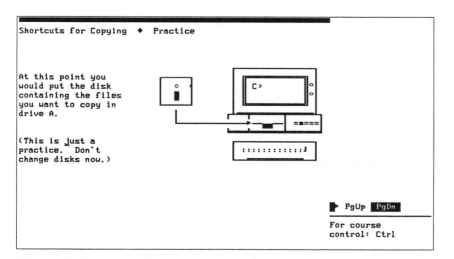

Figure 10.2   (continued). Note that the label "Steps" has appeared at the top of this screen to signal users that they are reading the steps of the procedure they are about to practice.

```
Shortcuts for Copying  ◆  Practice


At this point you
would put the disk
containing the files                    o            C >                o
you want to copy in                     ▮
drive A.
                                        ┌─────────┐   ==▮====
(This is just a
practice.  Don't                        │ ::::::::::::┘ │
change disks now.)



                                                  ▶ PgUp  PgDn

                                                  For course
                                                  control: Ctrl
```

Figure 10.2   (continued). The label "Practice" tells users that they are now in a hands-on practice session. Note how the designers are able to show users where to insert a disk by using simple two-dimensional images.

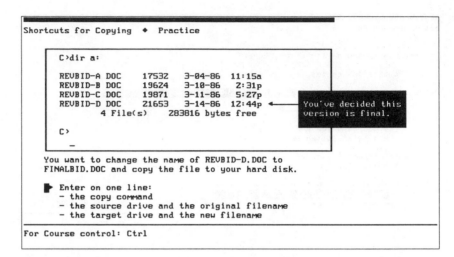

```
Shortcuts for Copying  ◆  Practice


    C>dir a:

    REVBID-A DOC     17532    3-04-86   11:15a
    REVBID-B DOC     19624    3-10-86    2:31p
    REVBID-C DOC     19871    3-11-86    5:27p
    REVBID-D DOC     21653    3-14-86   12:44p  ◀─── You've decided this
              4 File(s)      283816 bytes free        version is final.

    C>
    _


    You want to change the name of REVBID-D.DOC to
    FINALBID.DOC and copy the file to your hard disk.

  ▶ Enter on one line:
     - the copy command
     - the source drive and the original filename
     - the target drive and the new filename

Для Course control: Ctrl
```

Figure 10.2 (continued). This screen brings users back to the scenario and begins the actual practice. Note that the pointer has changed location from the previous screens. Now it signals users to follow the instruction.

```
Shortcuts for Copying  ◆  Practice


    REVBID-A DOC     17532    3-04-86   11:15a
    REVBID-B DOC     19624    3-10-86    2:31p
    REVBID-C DOC     19871    3-11-86    5:27p
    REVBID-D DOC     21653    3-14-86   12:44p
              4 File(s)      283816 bytes free

    C>copy a:revbid-d.doc c:finalbid.doc
            1 File(s) copied

    C>_

    Your file was copied.

  ▶ Now check drive C to see the file listed
    under its new name.



For Course control: Ctrl
```

Figure 10.2 (continued). This screen both shows and tells users that they've done the procedure correctly. (If they had pressed the wrong keys during the procedure, a message would have appeared telling them what they had done wrong and what they should do next.)

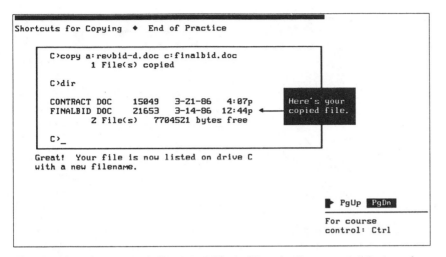

Figure 10.2 (continued). The label "End of Practice" appears at the top of the screen to let users know the hands-on session is over. Users get positive reinforcement not only from seeing the screen image change but also from reading the message of congratulations.

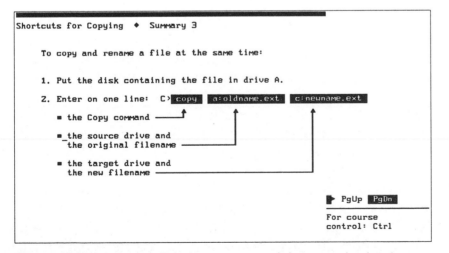

Figure 10.2 (continued). This summary screen brings users back to the "big picture," reminding them of the steps in the procedure they have just learned.

CHAPTER 11

Organizing Procedures Guides

A procedures guide is a collection of all the procedures users might want to perform with the software, along with any necessary descriptive text. The purpose of a procedures guide is to allow users to pick and choose those procedures they need to learn to get their work done.

You should group procedures according to function. Once you've established the major functional groups, you determine an appropriate sequence for those groups. You can arrange the groups in a chronological order that reflects the way readers use the program, in a most-used to least-used order, or in a simple-to-complex order.

For example, the following outline shows how you might group the procedures in a procedures guide for a word processing program. The modules follow a more or less chronological order, according to the sequence in which users will perform the procedures:

Basic Skills
   Starting the program
   Choosing commands and options
   Getting help
   Exiting from the program

File Management
   Creating new files
   Saving files
   Opening files
   Copying files
   Deleting files
   Combining files

Editing
   Copying text
   Moving text
   Deleting text
   Merging text from other files
   Using multiple windows to compare files

Formatting
   Changing fonts or type sizes
   Making characters bold, italic, or underlined
   Indenting paragraphs
   Aligning paragraphs
   Changing line spacing

Laying Out Pages
   Changing margins
   Adding headers or footers
   Adding page numbers
   Using multiple columns
   Adding lines or boxes
   Controlling page breaks

Printing
   Changing printer settings
   Previewing the printed pages
   Printing multiple copies
   Printing specific pages
   Printing form letters

For a data base program, you might begin with the most-used features, then move on to the least-used features:

Setting Up the Data Base
Entering Data
   Typing new data
   Entering data in form view
   Entering data in table view
   Importing data from another program
   Saving and loading files
Changing the Default Settings
   Changing the column width
   Changing the number format
   Changing the text format
Sorting
Printing
   Limiting the range of records to print
   Adding page numbers
   Printing in portrait or landscape mode
Reporting
   Using the default report design
   Creating your own reports
   Printing reports
Linking One Table to Another
Exporting Data Base Records
Recording Macros
Writing Program Scripts

In a computerized drafting program, you might arrange procedures to begin with the simplest tasks, then move on to the most complex:

Basic Drawing Skills
   Drawing lines
   Drawing circles
   Drawing squares

> Drawing Options
> > Creating arcs
> > Drawing curved shapes
> > Filling shapes
>
> Advanced Techniques
> > Rotating an object
> > Adding perspective
> > Creating an exploded view

You'll want to choose the arrangement that's most useful for your particular audience.

GUIDELINES FOR PROCEDURES GUIDES

To create an effective procedures guide, follow these guidelines:

O Organize the guide and group the procedures to reflect the way readers will use the program. For example, group together all procedures that enter information, all procedures that edit information, and so forth. Then organize the guide so that you list the procedures for entering information before you list the procedures for editing that information.

O Include all procedures, even those that you covered previously in a tutorial. (Never force users to refer to the tutorial once they've completed it.)

O Include all the information needed to successfully complete each procedure.

BASIC ORGANIZATIONS FOR MODULES IN A PROCEDURES GUIDE

All documentation is composed of modules. In a procedures guide, each procedure—along with any necessary explanatory text—makes up an individual module. Grouping these procedure modules provides the organization for the procedures guide as a whole. But along with deciding how to organize the guide, you need to decide how to organize each procedure module within the guide so the modules will be consistent. For example, you might structure a module like this:

   I. Heading (name of procedure)

   II. Introductory Paragraph(s)
      A. Basic concepts and definitions (as needed)
      B. Description of assumed conditions
      C. Cautions (as needed)

   III. Procedure (numbered steps)

   IV. Cross-references to Other Related Procedures

Each module should answer these questions:

○ Who performs the procedure? (unless this is always the same person)

○ What conditions are assumed at the time the user begins the procedure?

○ Can differences in hardware, files, or the program's environment change the procedure?

○ What steps are involved?

○ What is the program's response (if any) to each step?

○ Is this procedure related to or affected by other procedures?

SAMPLE PROCEDURES GUIDES

In this section, you'll see samples from two procedures guides.

The first sample is part of the *Aldus SnapShot User Manual*, in which the main body of the manual (four chapters) is the procedures guide section. The chapters follow a simple-to-complex order:

Chapter 1: Welcome to SnapShot

Chapter 2: SnapShot Possibilities

Chapter 3: Using SnapShot

Chapter 4: Using SnapShot Images in Other Applications

Figure 11.1 focuses on a few pages from Chapter 3. This chapter is divided into several main groupings of procedure modules:

Getting help

Capturing an image

Modifying an image

Creating special effects with gray levels

Proofing an image

Configuring SnapShot

Modifying an image

SnapShot gives you many ways to modify your image. You can sharpen fuzzy images or soften high-contrast ones. Create a line drawing effect by outlining the edges in your image. Take a smile from one image and place it on someone in another image. Add an absent employee to your group photograph. Touch up a portrait, removing blemishes, darkening hair color, even changing a hairline or adding a hat. Scale an area up in size, work on the enlarged section in great detail, then reduce it again, keeping all your modifications.

You can modify your image any time after you freeze it, either before or after saving. But the advantage of saving the image first is that you can always go back to your saved version to start over if you don't like the modifications you've made.

You choose all of SnapShot's modification commands ("Enhance…," "Touch-up…," and "Scale image…") from the Image menu:

```
Image
 Acquire            ^A
 Video source...

 Contrast...
 Photometrics...

 Freeze             ^F

 Enhance...
 Touch up...        ▶      ── Modification
 Scale image...                commands

 Gray levels...
```

SnapShot's modifications can be categorized into two groups:

- Area effects

  These are effects that SnapShot automatically applies to an entire selected area of the image. Area effects include scale, filter color, reduce blur, sharpen, and outline edges.

- Brush effects

  These are effects that you apply to the image using a "paintbrush." Brush effects include lighten and darken, increase local contrast, blend, paint with patterns, and paint with gray levels.

3-12   *Modifying an image*

Figure 11.1. Pages of a Procedures Guide (from *Aldus SnapShot User Manual*). Note how the section begins with an introduction to the group of procedures. The procedure modules all have the same structure: procedure title, introductory text, procedure steps. The procedure modules (starting on page 152) also share the same format, with the introduction to the steps set off with a rule and the steps in bold type.

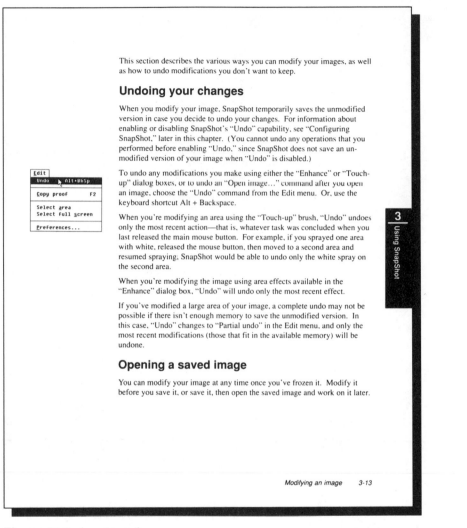

This section describes the various ways you can modify your images, as well as how to undo modifications you don't want to keep.

Undoing your changes

When you modify your image, SnapShot temporarily saves the unmodified version in case you decide to undo your changes. For information about enabling or disabling SnapShot's "Undo" capability, see "Configuring SnapShot," later in this chapter. (You cannot undo any operations that you performed before enabling "Undo," since SnapShot does not save an unmodified version of your image when "Undo" is disabled.)

To undo any modifications you make using either the "Enhance" or "Touch-up" dialog boxes, or to undo an "Open image…" command after you open an image, choose the "Undo" command from the Edit menu. Or, use the keyboard shortcut Alt + Backspace.

When you're modifying an area using the "Touch-up" brush, "Undo" undoes only the most recent action—that is, whatever task was concluded when you last released the main mouse button. For example, if you sprayed one area with white, released the mouse button, then moved to a second area and resumed spraying, SnapShot would be able to undo only the white spray on the second area.

When you're modifying the image using area effects available in the "Enhance" dialog box, "Undo" will undo only the most recent effect.

If you've modified a large area of your image, a complete undo may not be possible if there isn't enough memory to save the unmodified version. In this case, "Undo" changes to "Partial undo" in the Edit menu, and only the most recent modifications (those that fit in the available memory) will be undone.

Opening a saved image

You can modify your image at any time once you've frozen it. Modify it before you save it, or save it, then open the saved image and work on it later.

Modifying an image   3-13

Figure 11.1 (continued).

To open a saved image:

1. Choose "Open image..." from the File menu.

If you have not frozen the image on the screen, SnapShot asks: "Freeze this image?" Click "Cancel" to stop the "Open" command, or click "OK" to freeze the image and proceed to open a new one.

Scroll the list box to find the name of the image you want. If necessary, change to a different directory or disk drive.

2. If you need more information about an image, click the name of the image, then click "Get Info."

The information you saved with your image is displayed. For more information about saving an image along with descriptive information, see "Saving the image," earlier in this chapter.

Click "Get Info" to see the information
you saved with the image

3. Click "OK" to return to the "Open image" dialog box.

4. In the "Open image" dialog box, click the name of the image, then click "Open."

If you've opened a full-screen image, the image appears on the video monitor and the title bar of the SnapShot window changes to "SnapShot—Frozen."

If you've opened an image that's less than full-screen, an arrow appears on the video monitor. When you hold down the main mouse button, you'll see a box the size of the image. Position the box where you want the image to be, then release the mouse button and the image appears on the monitor. The title bar changes to "SnapShot—Modified."

3-14   *Modifying an image*

Figure 11.1 (continued).

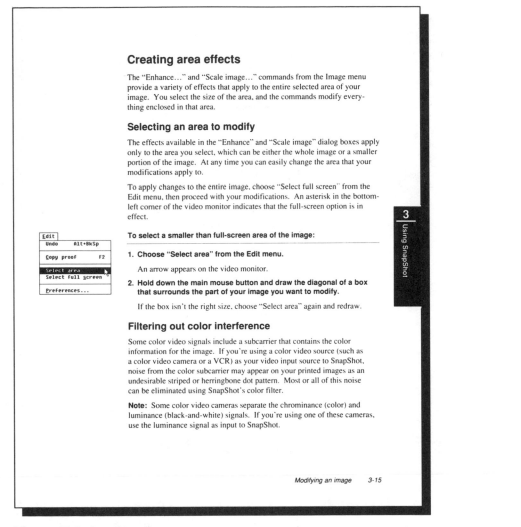

Creating area effects

The "Enhance..." and "Scale image..." commands from the Image menu provide a variety of effects that apply to the entire selected area of your image. You select the size of the area, and the commands modify everything enclosed in that area.

Selecting an area to modify

The effects available in the "Enhance" and "Scale image" dialog boxes apply only to the area you select, which can be either the whole image or a smaller portion of the image. At any time you can easily change the area that your modifications apply to.

To apply changes to the entire image, choose "Select full screen" from the Edit menu, then proceed with your modifications. An asterisk in the bottom-left corner of the video monitor indicates that the full-screen option is in effect.

To select a smaller than full-screen area of the image:

1. **Choose "Select area" from the Edit menu.**

   An arrow appears on the video monitor.

2. **Hold down the main mouse button and draw the diagonal of a box that surrounds the part of your image you want to modify.**

   If the box isn't the right size, choose "Select area" again and redraw.

Filtering out color interference

Some color video signals include a subcarrier that contains the color information for the image. If you're using a color video source (such as a color video camera or a VCR) as your video input source to SnapShot, noise from the color subcarrier may appear on your printed images as an undesirable striped or herringbone dot pattern. Most or all of this noise can be eliminated using SnapShot's color filter.

Note: Some color video cameras separate the chrominance (color) and luminance (black-and-white) signals. If you're using one of these cameras, use the luminance signal as input to SnapShot.

Modifying an image   3-15

Figure 11.1 (continued).

Patterns caused by
color interference

"Filter color" command
removes interference
patterns

To filter out color interference:

1. **Choose either "Select area" or "Select full screen" from the Edit menu to select the area you want to filter.**

   For more information about selecting an area, see the previous section, "Selecting an area to modify."

2. **Choose "Enhance…" from the Image menu.**

3. **Under "Color" in the "Enhance" dialog box, click "Filter."**

   On the screen, you can watch the progress of the filtering in the area you've selected. To stop the filtering before it's complete, click the secondary mouse button.

4. **If noise still remains, click "Filter" again.**

   Noise is reduced further each time you click "Filter."

3-16   Modifying an image

Figure 11.1 (continued).

5. **Either continue selecting from the "Enhance" dialog box, or double-click in the top-left corner of the dialog box to close it.**

Reducing blur

If you've captured your image from a moving subject or moved the camera at the moment of capture, your image may be flickering or blurred. The standard video monitor displays two interlaced fields of view every 1/60th of a second. Normally, the two images are identical, and your eye sees only a single image. But if movement occurs during the moment you freeze the image using the "Freeze" command, these two fields will not be identical, and your eye will detect the difference as flicker or blur.

You may be able to improve a blurred image by using SnapShot's "Motion Stop" option in the "Enhance" dialog box. However, some detail may be lost because SnapShot averages between adjacent lines on the display.

Note: Cameras with a high shutter speed (e.g., 1/1000 sec) will usually capture moving images without blur.

To reduce blur:

1. **Choose either "Select area" or "Select full screen" from the Edit menu to select the area you want.**

   For more information about selecting an area, see "Selecting an area to modify," earlier in this chapter.

2. **Choose "Enhance..." from the Image menu.**

Modifying an image   3-17

Figure 11.1 (continued).

3. Under "Motion" in the "Enhance" dialog box, click "Stop."

On the screen, you can watch the progress of the operation in the area you've selected. To stop the operation before it's complete, click the secondary mouse button.

4. Either continue selecting from the "Enhance" dialog box, or double-click in the top-left corner of the dialog box to close it.

Sharpening the image

You can sharpen your image using SnapShot's "Sharpening" options in the "Enhance" dialog box. Sharpening increases the contrast between adjacent pixels and smooths out low-contrast areas, giving edges and textures more definition.

If you've captured your image from a color video source and you intend to remove the color interference patterns by filtering, use the color filter *before* sharpening. Sharpening will enhance the undesirable patterns introduced by color signals. In addition, color filtering causes a slight loss of sharpness that can be improved by using the "Sharpening" options. For more information about color interference, see "Filtering out color interference," earlier in this chapter.

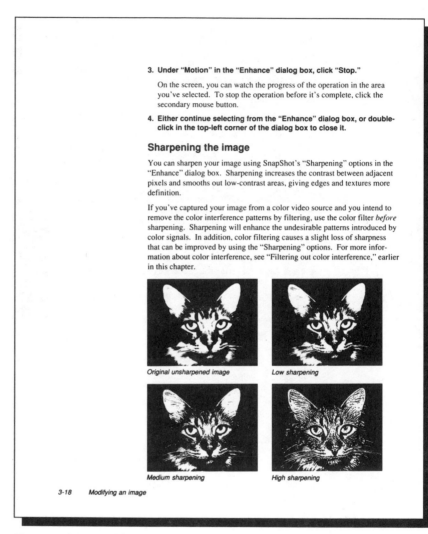

Original unsharpened image   Low sharpening

Medium sharpening   High sharpening

3-18   Modifying an image

Figure 11.1 (continued).

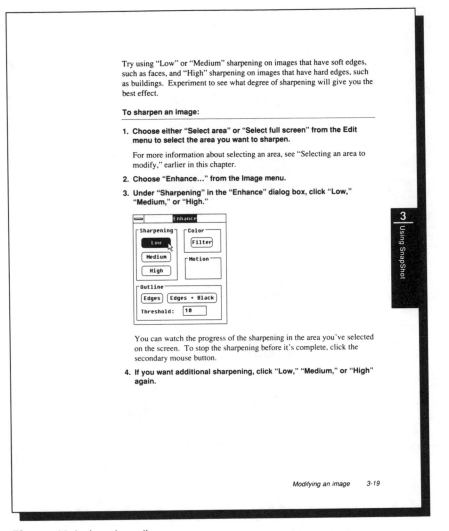

Try using "Low" or "Medium" sharpening on images that have soft edges, such as faces, and "High" sharpening on images that have hard edges, such as buildings. Experiment to see what degree of sharpening will give you the best effect.

To sharpen an image:

1. **Choose either "Select area" or "Select full screen" from the Edit menu to select the area you want to sharpen.**

   For more information about selecting an area, see "Selecting an area to modify," earlier in this chapter.

2. **Choose "Enhance..." from the Image menu.**

3. **Under "Sharpening" in the "Enhance" dialog box, click "Low," "Medium," or "High."**

   You can watch the progress of the sharpening in the area you've selected on the screen. To stop the sharpening before it's complete, click the secondary mouse button.

4. **If you want additional sharpening, click "Low," "Medium," or "High" again.**

Modifying an image   3-19

Figure 11.1 (continued).

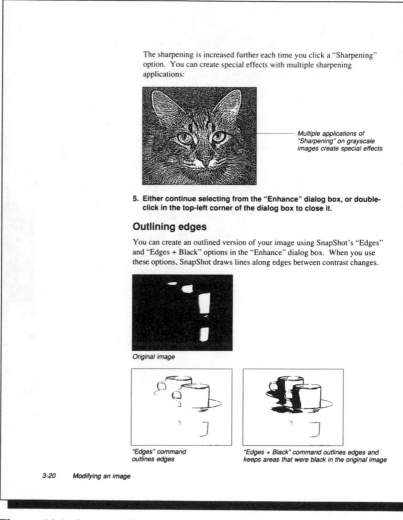

The sharpening is increased further each time you click a "Sharpening" option. You can create special effects with multiple sharpening applications:

Multiple applications of "Sharpening" on grayscale images create special effects

5. **Either continue selecting from the "Enhance" dialog box, or double-click in the top-left corner of the dialog box to close it.**

Outlining edges

You can create an outlined version of your image using SnapShot's "Edges" and "Edges + Black" options in the "Enhance" dialog box. When you use these options, SnapShot draws lines along edges between contrast changes.

Original image

"Edges" command outlines edges

"Edges + Black" command outlines edges and keeps areas that were black in the original image

3-20   Modifying an image

Figure 11.1 (continued).

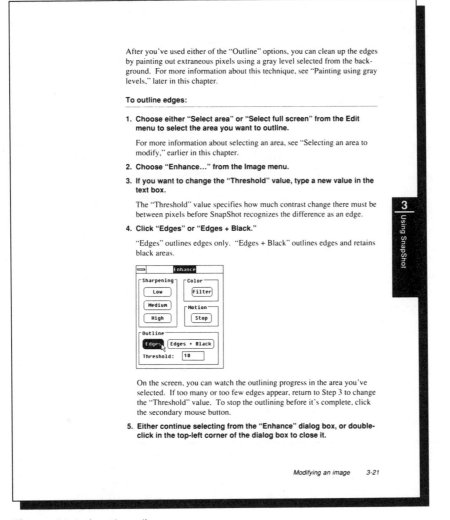

After you've used either of the "Outline" options, you can clean up the edges by painting out extraneous pixels using a gray level selected from the background. For more information about this technique, see "Painting using gray levels," later in this chapter.

To outline edges:

1. **Choose either "Select area" or "Select full screen" from the Edit menu to select the area you want to outline.**

   For more information about selecting an area, see "Selecting an area to modify," earlier in this chapter.

2. **Choose "Enhance..." from the Image menu.**

3. **If you want to change the "Threshold" value, type a new value in the text box.**

   The "Threshold" value specifies how much contrast change there must be between pixels before SnapShot recognizes the difference as an edge.

4. **Click "Edges" or "Edges + Black."**

   "Edges" outlines edges only. "Edges + Black" outlines edges and retains black areas.

   On the screen, you can watch the outlining progress in the area you've selected. If too many or too few edges appear, return to Step 3 to change the "Threshold" value. To stop the outlining before it's complete, click the secondary mouse button.

5. **Either continue selecting from the "Enhance" dialog box, or double-click in the top-left corner of the dialog box to close it.**

Modifying an image   3-21

Figure 11.1 (continued).

The next sample is from a more technical, less art-intensive manual, *R:BASE for DOS User's Manual*. This manual has a most-used to least-used organization of procedure groups:

Chapter 1: R:BASE Fundamentals
Chapter 2: Database Definition
Chapter 3: Data Entry and Modification
Chapter 4: Building Forms Using Forms EXPRESS
Chapter 5: Data Output Using R:BASE Commands
Chapter 6: Data Output Using Reports EXPRESS
Chapter 7: Creating, Combining, and Appending Tables
Chapter 8: System Maintenance
Chapter 9: Customizing R:BASE

We're concentrating on a few pages from Chapter 8, "System Maintenance." The chapter groups the procedure modules as follows:

Working with Files, Directories, and Drives in R:BASE
Backing Up and Recovering a Database
Transferring Data from One Database to Another
Compressing Your Database
Database Security

Figure 11.2 shows some of the procedure modules in the "Backing Up and Recovering a Database" section.

BACKING UP A WHOLE DATABASE

Backing Up with BACKUP

The BACKUP command copies your database into a different format than your *.rbf* database files. BACKUP creates an input file that contains the R:BASE commands needed to define the database and load data into it, followed by the data itself in ASCII delimited format. The file also includes forms, reports, rules, and views in the database.

With BACKUP, you can back up the database with a single command. Your backup copy consists of one file rather than several and you can restore the database with a single RESTORE command. If you have a hard disk and are backing up your database to a floppy disk and the backup is too large for one disk, BACKUP allows you to change disks. Although your backup may be on several disks, it is still one file, so you cannot recover only part of the database from your backup copy. Even if your database will fit on one disk, you may want to back up the structure and the data separately as described in ''Backing Up the Database in Parts'' later in this chapter. This way, if only part of your database is damaged, you can recover just that part from your backup.

This is the syntax for the BACKUP command:

```
           ┌─ALL──────┐
BACKUP ─┤  DATA        ├─┬─ FOR tblname ─┬──────────────────  ...
           └─STRUCTURE─┘ │               └─ USING ─┬─ collist ─┐
                                                    └─ ALL ────┘
```

```
  ...   ┌─ SORTED BY collist ─┬─┬─ WHERE condlist ─┘
        └─ ORDER BY collist ──┘ └
```

To back up your database to a single floppy disk or to a directory on a hard disk using BACKUP ALL, follow these steps:

1. Use the OPEN command to open the database you want to back up; enter the user password if one is required.

2. Set NULL to -0-.

Figure 11.2. Pages in a Procedures Guide (from *R:BASE for DOS User's Manual*). Note how the procedural modules all have the same structure: procedure title, introductory text, procedure steps. Procedures are set off with numbered steps, with examples and program responses described beneath the steps.

3. Prepare the destination of the backup copy. If you are backing up your database to another directory on your hard disk, make sure the directory exists or create it using the MKDIR command. If you have a hard disk and are backing up your database to a floppy disk, insert a blank, formatted disk in the floppy disk drive.

4. Use the OUTPUT command to direct output to a file. For example:

   OUTPUT dbname.bup

   To store the file elsewhere than the current drive and directory, specify the drive and directory with the file name. For example, *c:\backup\dbname.bup* or *a:dbname.bup*.

   To make sure your backup is proceeding correctly, enter *WITH SCREEN* after *dbname.bup* on the command line. R:BASE will display the information being written to the backup file on the screen.

5. Use BACKUP ALL to back up the database to the file:

   BACKUP ALL

   If your database is large, backing it up can take some minutes. Wait until the R> prompt appears again before you type another command.

   If the disk becomes full while R:BASE is backing up your database, R:BASE prompts you to insert another disk:

   Change disks and press [ENTER] to continue—Press [ESC] to cancel

   If you have a hard disk and are backing up your database to floppy disks, remove the current disk and label it with the name of the database, the date, and its order in the backup (for example, *1* for the first disk). Then insert another blank, formatted floppy disk in the drive and press [ENTER] to continue backing up the database.

   If you are backing up your database to another directory on your hard disk and the disk becomes full, press [ESC] to cancel the BACKUP command. Erase some files from your hard disk to make room for the backup file, or back up the database to floppy disks.

6. When the R> prompt reappears, use the OUTPUT command again to close the output file by redirecting the output to the screen, the printer, or another file. For example:

   OUTPUT SCREEN

   If you need to remove the backup disk before continuing your work, close the output file by entering OUTPUT SCREEN before removing the disk. If you do not, the last buffer of information will not be written to the file and your backup will be incomplete.

Recovering with RESTORE

To recover a database from a backup copy created with BACKUP ALL, follow these steps:

1. To recover the database to a directory other than the current directory (the one you are in now), change to the directory using the CHDIR command.

Figure 11.2 (continued).

2. If any *.rbf* files of the damaged database remain, rename them using the RENAME command. Later, after you confirm that your database has been successfully restored, delete the damaged *.rbf* files with the ERASE command.

3. If you are recovering the database from a floppy disk, insert the disk into the floppy disk drive. If there is more than one backup disk, insert the first one.

4. Use the RESTORE command to recover the database. For example:

    RESTORE dbname.bup

    If the file is elsewhere than the current drive and directory, specify the drive and directory with the file name. For example, *c:\backup\dbname.bup* or *a:dbname.bup*.

5. R:BASE prompts you to confirm. Press [Y] to restore the disk, [N] to skip it.

    R:BASE begins restoring your database. While it does so, R:BASE displays the same messages as when you first define a database using the DEFINE command and load data into it using the LOAD command:

    Begin R:BASE Database Definition
    End R:BASE Database Definition
    Begin R:BASE Data Loading
    End R:BASE Data Loading
    Switching INPUT back to KEYBOARD

    The last message is one that usually appears when R:BASE finishes running a command file.

    Depending on the size of your database, recovering it can take anywhere from a few minutes to several hours. Wait until the R> prompt appears again before typing another command.

    If you are recovering a database from multiple floppy disks, RESTORE prompts for each disk.

BACKING UP THE DATABASE IN PARTS

If you have a hard disk and your database is too large to fit on one disk, if you want to back up some tables but not others, or if you want the flexibility of being able to recover a database table by table, you can back up the database in parts.

Should your database be damaged, you may not have to recover the entire database. For example, if you accidentally delete rows from a table, you need only recover that table. If R:BASE was interrupted in the middle of an operation, the database may be partially intact.

If you think your database is not entirely ruined, first try to find out what parts of it are usable. Try to open the database. If it opens, try using the COMPUTE command to count the number of rows in a column from one of the tables. For example:

    COMPUTE COUNT colname FROM tblname

If the computation does not return the number of rows you expect, the data in that table may have been lost. By testing the other tables that should have data, you will be able to determine the extent of the damage. Another way to test for damage is to try selecting information from a table you suspect is damaged.

Figure 11.2 (continued).

Once you have identified the tables that are damaged and in need of recovery, restore the individual tables from your backup copy.

If you are using a computer with a dual 3.5-inch floppy disk system, you can use the UNLOAD command to back up a part of your database. See "Transferring Data from One Database to Another" later in this chapter.

Backing Up a Table

You can back up a table into a single file by specifying a table name with BACKUP ALL.

1. Use the OPEN command to open the database you want to back up; enter the user password if one is required.

2. Set NULL to -0-.

3. Prepare the destination of the backup copy. If you are backing up your database to another directory on your hard disk, make sure the directory exists or create it using the MKDIR command. If you are backing up your database to a floppy disk, insert a blank, formatted disk in the floppy disk drive.

4. Use OUTPUT to direct output to a file. For example:

   OUTPUT tblname.bup

   To store the file elsewhere than the current drive and directory, specify the drive and directory with the file name. For example, *c:\backup\tblname.bup* or *a:tblname.bup*.

   To make sure your backup is proceeding correctly, enter *WITH SCREEN* after *dbname.bup* on the command line. R:BASE will display the information being written to the backup file on the screen.

5. Use BACKUP ALL to back up the table to the file:

   BACKUP ALL FOR tblname

   If your table is large, backing it up can take a few minutes. Wait until the R> prompt appears again before you type another command.

   If the disk becomes full, BACKUP prompts you to insert another disk. Insert the next disk and press [ENTER] to continue the backup. If you are backing up to your hard disk, press [ESC] to cancel the BACKUP command. Make room on the disk, then start again at step 4.

6. When the R> prompt reappears, use the OUTPUT command again to close the output file by redirecting the output to the screen, the printer, or another file. For example:

   OUTPUT SCREEN

   If you need to remove the backup disk before continuing your work, close the output file by entering OUTPUT SCREEN before removing the disk. If you do not, the last buffer of information will not be written to the file and your backup will be incomplete.

Figure 11.2 (continued).

Recovering a Table

If the table you are recovering from your backup still exists in your database, the data from the backup is appended to any data that remains in the table, possibly duplicating some rows. To prevent duplicate rows, delete all rows from the table or remove the table from the database before recovering it from your backup. As an alternative, you can recover the table and then remove duplicate rows by using the DELETE DUPLICATES command.

If the table you are recovering might contain usable data not in your backup, first rename the table, then recover it from your most recent backup and append the usable data from the damaged table.

Because the backup file contains R:BASE commands to define the structure of the table, which is already defined in the existing database, some error messages will appear as R:BASE tries to define columns that already exist. These messages do not mean that R:BASE cannot recover the table. However, if your computer beeps when R:BASE displays an error message, you may want to use the SET BELL OFF command to silence it.

To recover a table from a backup copy created with BACKUP ALL, follow these steps:

1. Open the database that contains the table you want to recover.

2. If you are recovering the table from a floppy disk, insert the disk into the floppy disk drive.

3. Use the RESTORE command to recover the table. For example:

    RESTORE tblname.bup

    If the file is elsewhere than the current drive and directory, specify the drive and directory with the file name. For example *c:\backup\tblname.bup* or *a:tblname.bup*.

    R:BASE begins recovering the table and displays this message once for each column it tries to redefine:

    -ERROR- Existing columns cannot be redefined

    If your table is large, recovering it can take a few minutes. Wait until the R> prompt appears again before typing another command.

Backing Up Database Structure and Data Separately

Backing up database structure and data separately provides a great deal of flexibility in recovering the database. For example, if you make unintentional changes to a table, you can recover just the data from a backup file created with BACKUP DATA for that table. If your entire database is lost, however, you must reassemble the database from all your backup files rather than from a single file.

Figure 11.2 (continued).

166   ORGANIZING SOFTWARE DOCUMENTATION

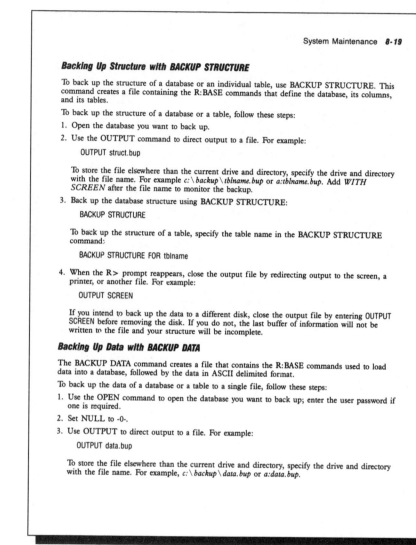

Backing Up Structure with BACKUP STRUCTURE

To back up the structure of a database or an individual table, use BACKUP STRUCTURE. This command creates a file containing the R:BASE commands that define the database, its columns, and its tables.

To back up the structure of a database or a table, follow these steps:

1. Open the database you want to back up.

2. Use the OUTPUT command to direct output to a file. For example:

   OUTPUT struct.bup

   To store the file elsewhere than the current drive and directory, specify the drive and directory with the file name. For example *c:\backup\tblname.bup* or *a:tblname.bup*. Add *WITH SCREEN* after the file name to monitor the backup.

3. Back up the database structure using BACKUP STRUCTURE:

   BACKUP STRUCTURE

   To back up the structure of a table, specify the table name in the BACKUP STRUCTURE command:

   BACKUP STRUCTURE FOR tblname

4. When the R> prompt reappears, close the output file by redirecting output to the screen, a printer, or another file. For example:

   OUTPUT SCREEN

   If you intend to back up the data to a different disk, close the output file by entering OUTPUT SCREEN before removing the disk. If you do not, the last buffer of information will not be written to the file and your structure will be incomplete.

Backing Up Data with BACKUP DATA

The BACKUP DATA command creates a file that contains the R:BASE commands used to load data into a database, followed by the data in ASCII delimited format.

To back up the data of a database or a table to a single file, follow these steps:

1. Use the OPEN command to open the database you want to back up; enter the user password if one is required.

2. Set NULL to -0-.

3. Use OUTPUT to direct output to a file. For example:

   OUTPUT data.bup

   To store the file elsewhere than the current drive and directory, specify the drive and directory with the file name. For example, *c:\backup\data.bup* or *a:data.bup*.

Figure 11.2   (continued).

8-20 User's Manual

To make sure your backup is proceeding correctly, enter *WITH SCREEN* after *dbname.bup* on the command line. R:BASE will display the information being written to the backup file on the screen.

4. Use BACKUP DATA to back up the data to the file:

   BACKUP DATA

To back up data from a table, include the table name with the BACKUP DATA command:

   BACKUP DATA FOR tblname

5. When the R> prompt reappears, close the output file by redirecting output to the screen, a printer, or another file. For example:

   OUTPUT SCREEN

If you need to remove the backup disk before continuing your work, close the output file by entering OUTPUT SCREEN before removing the disk. If you do not, the last buffer of information will not be written to the file and your data will be incomplete.

Backing Up Data Selectively

To back up selected data from a table, you can use a WHERE clause with the BACKUP command to limit the rows you back up. For example, if your table contains dated transactions, you might selectively back up old transactions and then delete them from the database.

To back up selected data from a table, follow these steps:

1. Use the OPEN command to open the database you want to back up; enter the user password if one is required.

2. Set NULL to -0-.

3. Use the OUTPUT command to direct output to the first file to hold your data. For example:

   OUTPUT transx.bup

To make sure your backup is proceeding correctly, enter *WITH SCREEN* after *dbname.bup* on the command line. R:BASE will display the information being written to the backup file on the screen.

4. Back up the data from the table. For example:

   BACKUP DATA FOR customer WHERE tdate LE 6/1/87

This WHERE clause limits the data that is backed up to rows where *tdate* is less than or equal to 6/1/87.

If the disk becomes full, BACKUP prompts you to change disks. Insert the next disk and press [ENTER] to continue the backup. Press [ESC] to cancel the BACKUP command.

Figure 11.2 (continued).

5. When you are finished backing up the data, close the output file by redirecting the output to a printer, the screen, or another file. For example:

```
OUTPUT SCREEN
```

If you need to remove the backup disk before continuing your work, close the output file by entering OUTPUT SCREEN before removing the disk. If you do not, the last buffer of information will not be written to the file and your data will be incomplete.

Recovering a Database or Table from Multiple Backup Files

To recover a database from backup files created with BACKUP STRUCTURE and BACKUP DATA, follow these steps:

1. To recover the database to a directory other than the current directory (the one you are in now), change to the directory using the CHDIR command.

2. If any *.rbf* files of the damaged database remain, rename them using the RENAME command. Later, after you confirm that your database has been successfully restored, delete the damaged *.rbf* files with the ERASE command. If you are recovering a table and the damaged table is still in the database, rename it with the RENAME command. After confirming that it has been successfully restored, remove it using the REMOVE TABLE command.

3. If you are recovering from a floppy disk, insert the disk into the floppy disk drive.

4. Use the RESTORE command to recover the database or table structure from the file you created with BACKUP STRUCTURE. For example:

```
RESTORE struct.bup
```

If the file is elsewhere than the current drive and directory, specify the drive and directory with the file name. For example, *c:\backup\struct.bup* or *a:struct.bup*.

5. Use the RESTORE command to recover the data from the file or files you created with BACKUP DATA. For example:

```
RESTORE data.bup
```

Use as many RESTORE commands as you need to recover data from each backup file.

Creating a Date-stamped Backup

If you make many entries to one or more tables in your database each day, you may want to back up each day's entries to a separate file.

If your table has a date column that is filled in with the current date for each entry, you can select the rows to back up by the value in the date column. An example of a table with a date column is *transx* in the *concomp* database, which has the column *tdate*.

To back up one day's entries to a backup file:

Figure 11.2 (continued).

CHAPTER **12**

Organizing
Reference Materials

Reference materials are catalogs of commands, functions, key assignments, and/or messages. Reference materials are built on these underlying assumptions: that users know which tasks they want to accomplish, that they are familiar with the program interface, and that they already know how to use the program. Reference materials usually contain more comprehensive technical information than any other type of documentation. The purpose of reference materials is to give experienced users quick access to details.

You usually divide reference materials into logical sections, like this:

    I. Commands

  II. Key assignments

 III. Messages

Reference materials can be assembled into one complete manual or a section in a combination manual.

GUIDELINES FOR REFERENCE MATERIALS

Here are some general guidelines for reference materials:

○ Organize each section—commands, key assignments, or messages—in the way that's most effective for that particular type of section.

○ If your reference material describes a problem (a frequent occurrence when listing error messages), be sure to include the solution, unless it's obvious.

○ Use a consistent format for each module in a reference section.

WAYS TO ORGANIZE SECTIONS IN REFERENCE MATERIALS

You can choose one of the following methods to arrange the sections in reference materials:

○ Match the interface (by menu or by screen).

○ Use alphabetical or numerical order.

○ Group information according to function.

Although the format within each section of a reference manual should be consistent, the organization for each type of section can differ. For example, you might arrange the catalog of commands in a manual according to menu and then arrange the list of error messages alphabetically by the first word of the message and the list of key assignments by function.

If you can, it's a good idea to organize sections so they will match the program interface. For example, consider a catalog of commands. If users access commands by choosing them from a menu, it's a good idea to group commands by menu. In a program that requires users to fill in fields on the screen, you can group the fields by screen, then list fields in the order in which they appear (top to bottom, left to right). Include a picture of each screen at the beginning of the section so readers can easily follow the sequence of information.

However, if users choose the items listed in your reference section in no particular order, you'll probably want to arrange the information in alphabetical order. Alphabetical order is appropriate for a listing of messages or for a catalog of commands where users type the command of their choice at a prompt or mix and match commands to create a program.

Once you've decided which sections to include in your reference manual and how to best organize each of them, you then need to decide how to organize the modules in each of these sections. Your readers don't want to wade through page after page of the manual to find the one bit of information they're looking for, so make sure you use a consistent format for each module in a section.

If you're describing an application in which commands display dialog boxes, you might develop a format that looks like this:

   I. Command name

  II. Description of use

 III. Picture of dialog box

  IV. Description of dialog box options (in order in which they appear)
       A. Name of option
       B. Purpose of option
       C. Rules for entering information (if any)

   V. Cautions (if any)

  VI. Cross-references to related commands

SAMPLE ORGANIZATION FOR A LANGUAGE FUNCTION REFERENCE MODULE

If you're organizing a reference section for a language manual in which you'll list all the functions in alphabetical order, you might structure each module like this:

    I. Function name

   II. Description of use

  III. Examples of syntax

  IV. Description of switches, variables, and other options that can be used with the function

   V. Cautions (if any)

  VI. Return values and messages

 VII. Cross-references to other related functions

SAMPLE ORGANIZATION FOR A SCREEN-ORIENTED MODULE

When you document a program that requires users to fill in fields on a variety of screens, you might want to develop module structures like this:

    I. Screen name

   II. Description of general use of screen

  III. Description of fields (in the order in which they appear)
      A. Name of field
      B. Purpose of field
      C. Rules for entering information

  IV. Cautions (if any)

   V. Cross-references to other related screens and fields

SAMPLE ORGANIZATION FOR A MESSAGE REFERENCE MODULE

The better the wording of a message, the less explanation it needs, so it's always a good idea for documentation writers to be involved in formulating messages. Unfortunately, it's not always possible to create messages that explicitly state their own causes and solutions. So if all the on-screen messages for your program aren't self-explanatory, you'll need to provide more information to guide users.

The organization of your module might look like this:

I.   Message

II. Description of condition causing message (unless the message states the cause)

III. Description of how to solve the problem (unless the solution is obvious from the wording of the message)

SAMPLE REFERENCE MATERIALS

In this section you'll see samples from a variety of reference manuals.

Figure 12.1 shows two pages from the *AST Operating System* manual, which is an alphabetically arranged reference manual.

Figure 12.2 shows sample pages from the menu reference section of the *Xerox Ventura Publisher Reference Guide*.

Using MS-DOS

Type

Purpose:

Displays the contents of a text file on the screen.

Syntax:

type [*drive:*]*filename*

Comments:

You can use the **type** command to view a text file without modifying it. (Use **dir** to find the name of a file and **Edlin** to change the contents of a file.)

Note that when you use **type** to display a file that contains tabs, all the tabs are expanded to the current setting for tabs (generally eight spaces wide). Also, if you try to display a binary file or a file created by an application program, you may see strange characters on the screen, including bells, formfeeds, and escape-sequence symbols.

Examples:

If you want to display the contents of a file called *holiday.mar*, you would type the following command:

```
type holiday.mar
```

If the contents of the file you want to display are fairly long, you could use a command like this to display the file's contents one screen at a time:

```
type holiday.88 | more
```

3-136

Figure 12.1. Pages from a Command Reference Module Organized Alphabetically (from *AST Operating System Manual*). Note the consistent format of the two modules in this figure.

MS-DOS   Commands

Ver

Purpose:

Prints the MS-DOS version number.

Syntax:

ver

Comment:

If you want to know what version of MS-DOS you are using, type the **ver** command. The version number will then be displayed on your screen.

Example:

When you type the **ver** command, the following message is displayed:

```
MS-DOS Version 3.30
```

3-137

Figure 12.1 (continued).

FRAME MENU

Frame
Margins & Columns...
Sizing & Scaling...
Frame Typography...

Anchors & Captions...
Repeating Frame...

Vertical Rules...
Ruling Line Above...
Ruling Line Below...
Ruling Box Around...
Frame Background...

Image Settings...

Figure 5–36   Frame Menu.

The **Frame menu** controls the format of frames, as well as the page format (remember, the page is just another frame). Using the options in the Frame menu you can control margins, columns, ruling lines, frame sizing and scaling, frame typography, anchors and captions, background fill patterns, and image settings.

The page itself is like any other frame, except that Margin and Column settings for the page are stored in the style sheet file. All other frame settings are stored with the chapter file.

Changes made to any page affect all non-inserted pages (see **Insert/Remove pages** in the Chapter menu). Changes to each inserted page or changes to frames which you draw affect only that one page or frame.

Figure 12.2 Pages from a Command Reference Module Organized by Menu (from *Xerox Ventura Publisher Reference Guide*). Note that the section begins with a picture and description of the menu. This introduction is followed by a thorough description and discussion of each command on the menu. This figure shows four of these command reference modules.

Margins & columns

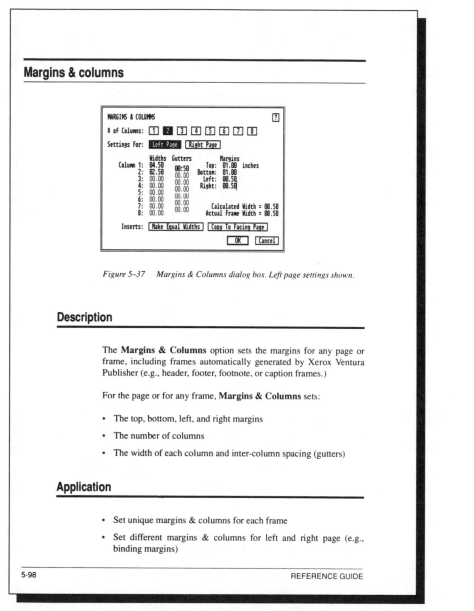

Figure 5–37   Margins & Columns dialog box. Left page settings shown.

Description

The **Margins & Columns** option sets the margins for any page or frame, including frames automatically generated by Xerox Ventura Publisher (e.g., header, footer, footnote, or caption frames.)

For the page or for any frame, **Margins & Columns** sets:

- The top, bottom, left, and right margins

- The number of columns

- The width of each column and inter-column spacing (gutters)

Application

- Set unique margins & columns for each frame

- Set different margins & columns for left and right page (e.g., binding margins)

 **Figure 12.2** (continued).

- Create complementary facing pages
- Move pictures within a frame

Operation

You can change the margins and number of columns for the page or any frame by following the basic steps which follow. For special situations, you must modify these steps slightly as described in the sections on the next several pages.

Basic steps

The basic steps given here allow you to create pages or frames which have the same widths for each column and the same margins for the left and right pages.

1) Select the Frame or Graphic mode.
2) Select the frame or page to be changed
3) Select the Margins & Columns option in the Frame menu. The **Margins & Columns** dialog box shown in Figure 5–37 appears.
4) Select the number of columns you want for the page or frame you selected.
5) Set each margin (top, bottom, left, right).
6) Set the first gutter space (the space between the first and second column).
7) Select **Make Equal Widths**.
8) Select **OK.**

Unequal column widths

You can also independently set each column's width as well as the gutter space between each column. This allows you to create unusual page designs where each column is different from the next.

1) Select the number of columns
2) Set each margin (top, bottom, left, right).
3) Set each column width
4) Set each gutter space.

After entering all information, but before selecting **OK**, make sure that the **Calculated Width** (which shows the current sum of left margin,

Figure 12.2 (continued).

right margin, column widths, and inter-column space) equals the **Actual Frame Width**. Xerox Ventura Publisher cannot do this for you because you have independent control over each setting, and it is therefore possible to create margin and column widths that don't equal the width of the page or frame.

☞ If the margin and column appearance on-screen do not match what you specified, check to make sure that Calculated Width equals Actual Frame Width.

Different left/right page margins

If **Double-Sided** was selected in the Page Layout option, each frame or page can have different margins, column widths, and gutter space for the left pages than for right pages. This is useful for creating binding margins and for making left pages which look different from right pages.

To set different margins and columns for left and right pages, follow the procedures for either equal or unequal column widths. However, *before selecting OK*, select **Settings For** the other page, then enter all settings for that page. *You must set both pages before you select OK or the settings for the one page will be automatically reflected to the other page.*

Copy to facing page

You can copy the left and right margin settings to the opposite page by selecting **Copy to facing page.** The margin settings automatically reflect, e.g., the right margin setting on one page becomes the left margin setting on the opposite page. The margin and column widths are not copied and must be explicitly set for both left and right pages.

Captions

Whenever you create a caption using the Anchors & Caption menu, a frame is automatically created for the new caption. This caption frame is automatically attached to the frame which contains the picture. The caption frame's settings can be changed independently by selecting it and setting its margins. The caption frame can also be selected and made larger or smaller.

☞ Hint: if you set different left/right page margins for a frame, use the Anchors & Captions option *after* you have set the frame's margins. Since the caption's initial margins are copied from the frame's margins, this eliminates the need to set the caption's margins.

Figure 12.2 (continued).

Header & footer frames

When you first create a header or footer, a frame is automatically created to hold it. This frame's margins are initially set to vertically center the text. To place the headers and footers in a different location within the header or footer frame you can change either the frame margins or change the header or footer paragraph tag's above, below, or left/right spacing. Changing the tag spacing is a better choice because it is stored in the style sheet and will therefore affect other documents in a similar manner.

Footnote frames

When you first create a footnote, a frame is automatically created to hold it. The frame's margins are initially set to vertically center the footnote text. However, like header & footer frames, you can change either the frame margins or the paragraph's above, below, or left/right spacing to change the footnote's location within a frame. You should change the paragraph tag's spacing whenever possible for the same reasons described in the previous paragraph.

Figure 12.2 (continued).

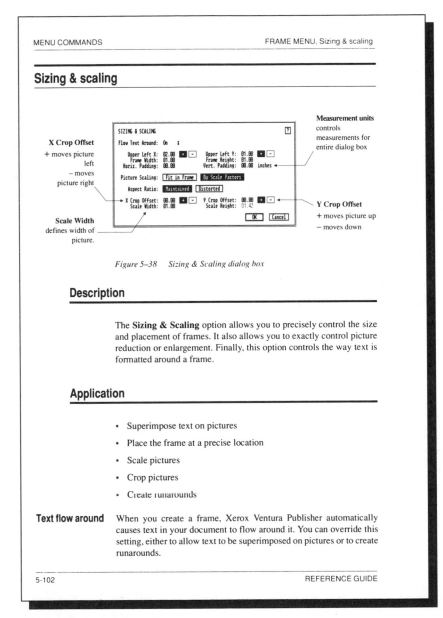

Sizing & scaling

X Crop Offset
+ moves picture left
− moves picture right

Measurement units
controls measurements for entire dialog box

Y Crop Offset
+ moves picture up
− moves down

Scale Width
defines width of picture.

Figure 5–38   Sizing & Scaling dialog box

Description

The **Sizing & Scaling** option allows you to precisely control the size and placement of frames. It also allows you to exactly control picture reduction or enlargement. Finally, this option controls the way text is formatted around a frame.

Application

- Superimpose text on pictures
- Place the frame at a precise location
- Scale pictures
- Crop pictures
- Create runarounds

Text flow around   When you create a frame, Xerox Ventura Publisher automatically causes text in your document to flow around it. You can override this setting, either to allow text to be superimposed on pictures or to create runarounds.

5-102   REFERENCE GUIDE

Figure 12.2 (continued).

To allow text to flow under a frame, turn **Flow Text Around** off. If the text contains tabs, text may not completely flow around frames.

☞   Use of this feature to make text wrap around pictures is covered in the **Frame** section in the Modes of Operation chapter.

Frame placement

Normally, you use the mouse to place frame's where you want them on a page. If, however, you want to position a frame with absolute precision, use the **Sizing & Scaling** option as follows:

1) Select the Frame mode

2) Select a frame

3) Select the **Sizing & Scaling** option in the Frame menu

4) Set the **Upper Left X** and **Upper Left Y** coordinates of the frame. These numbers refer to *the distance of the upper left corner of the frame from the upper left corner of the physical page* (Figure 5–39). The X coordinates are measured horizontally, the Y coordinates vertically.

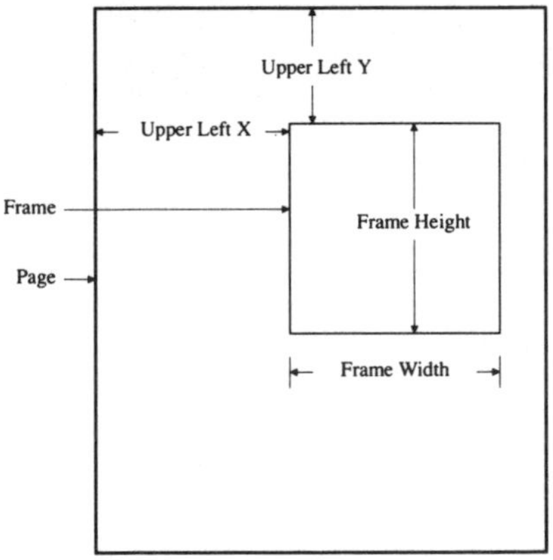

Figure 5–39   X and Y Frame placement defined

Figure 12.2 (continued).

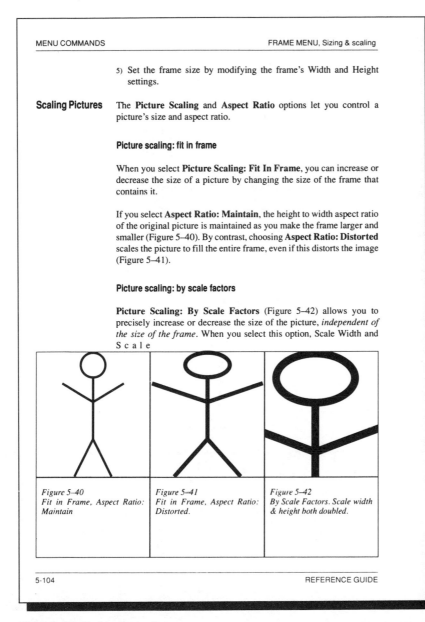

5) Set the frame size by modifying the frame's Width and Height settings.

Scaling Pictures   The **Picture Scaling** and **Aspect Ratio** options let you control a picture's size and aspect ratio.

Picture scaling: fit in frame

When you select **Picture Scaling: Fit In Frame**, you can increase or decrease the size of a picture by changing the size of the frame that contains it.

If you select **Aspect Ratio: Maintain**, the height to width aspect ratio of the original picture is maintained as you make the frame larger and smaller (Figure 5–40). By contrast, choosing **Aspect Ratio: Distorted** scales the picture to fill the entire frame, even if this distorts the image (Figure 5–41).

Picture scaling: by scale factors

Picture Scaling: By Scale Factors (Figure 5–42) allows you to precisely increase or decrease the size of the picture, *independent of the size of the frame*. When you select this option, Scale Width and S c a l e

Figure 5–40
Fit in Frame, Aspect Ratio: Maintain

Figure 5–41
Fit in Frame, Aspect Ratio: Distorted.

Figure 5–42
By Scale Factors. Scale width & height both doubled.

Figure 12.2 (continued).

Height control the width and height of the picture. For instance, selecting a Scale Width of 03.00 inches makes the picture exactly three inches wide.

When you select **Aspect Ratio: Maintained**, only the **Scale Width** can be set. The **Scale Height** is automatically increased or decreased as necessary to maintain the original aspect ratio of the picture. Neither scale width or height can exceed 27 inches.

When you select **Aspect Ratio: Distorted**, you can enter settings for both the **Scale Width** and **Scale Height**.

Cropping

Any picture can be cropped as follows:

- Select Frame or Graphic mode.

- Select the frame which contains the picture you wish to crop.

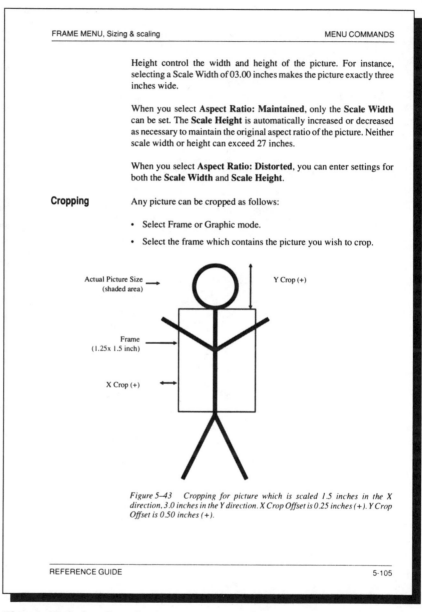

Figure 5–43   Cropping for picture which is scaled 1.5 inches in the X direction, 3.0 inches in the Y direction. X Crop Offset is 0.25 inches (+). Y Crop Offset is 0.50 inches (+).

Figure 12.2 (continued).

- Press and hold the **ALT** key.

- Place the mouse cursor in the center of the selected frame.

- Press and hold the mouse key and move the image to a new location within the frame.

Ignore any "clutter" that may be created as you crop the image. This will be eliminated when you release the mouse button.

You can also crop pictures by specifying the X (horizontal) and Y (vertical) amount to move the scaled picture relative to the frame (see Figure 5–43).

Padding

The **Padding** settings let you increase space around a frame to keep surrounding text from touching the side of a frame. You should set a vertical padding space equal to the body text inter-line spacing.

Padding is particularly important when you place pictures across column boundaries in multi-column documents. Use vertical padding to stop the vertical rules between columns from touching the top and bottom of the picture frame. Use horizontal padding to keep text in adjacent columns from touching the sides of the picture.

Custom size pages

The **Page Size & Layout** option in the Chapter menu offers a few fixed page sizes. If your document requires that you create custom size pages, use the **Frame Width** and **Frame Height** options in the **Sizing & Scaling** dialog box to create a custom size page. Custom pages must be smaller than the size selected in the **Page Size & Layout** option. To create custom size pages, follow these steps:

1) Select Frame mode.

2) Select the page.

3) Select the Sizing & Scaling menu.

4) Set the **Frame Width** and **Frame Height** to the size of the page you want to create.

5) Select **OK**.

Note that after you select OK, the custom page is positioned at the upper left corner of the page. If you want to center the custom page, adjust the **Upper Left X** and **Upper Left Y** values as necessary.

Figure 12.2 (continued).

FRAME MENU, Sizing & scaling   MENU COMMANDS

Scanned images   Scanned images look best when printed at exactly their original size. If this is not feasible, you can obtain the next best results by making the picture an exact integer multiple larger or smaller (e.g., 2X, 3X, 4X … or ½X, ⅓X, ¼X …). If you scale the picture by an odd amount, the picture may be marred by horizontal and vertical *moiré* lines. These result from the scaling process and are unavoidable.

You will see similar moiré lines when the image is displayed on the screen. These lines result from the difference between the resolution of the screen and the printer resolution. They are normal, do not affect printing, and should be ignored.

☞   To ensure that your scanned images are always scaled correctly, always select **Picture Scaling: By Scale Factors** and **Aspect Ratio: Maintained**. Immediately after you select By Scale Factors, the Scale Width will show the original size of the image. If you select OK at this point, the picture will print at exactly its original size, with the best possible quality. If you want to double or halve the size of the image, simply enter a Scale Width which is exactly twice or half the original picture width.

REFERENCE GUIDE   5-107

Figure 12.2 (continued).

Frame typography

```
┌─────────────────────────────────────────────┐
│ FRAME TYPOGRAPHY SETTINGS              [?]    │
│                                               │
│       Widows (Min Lines at Top):  Default  ↕  │
│   Orphans (Min Lines at Bottom):  Default  ↕  │
│               Column Balance:     Default  ↕  │
│      Move Down To 1st Baseline By: Default ↕  │
│               Pair Kerning:       Default  ↕  │
│                                               │
│                          [ OK ]  [ Cancel ]   │
└─────────────────────────────────────────────┘
```

Figure 5–44   Frame typography dialog box.

Description

The Frame Typography option overrides the global settings defined in the Chapter Typography menu. Settings will apply only to the frame or inserted page you have selected.

Application

The features in this menu option are used for sophisticated layouts to fine-tune the typography on a given page.

Operation

Follow these steps to use the Frame Typography option:

1) Select the Frame mode.

2) Select the Frame you wish to change.

3) Select the **Frame Typography** option in the Frame menu.

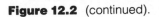

Figure 12.2 (continued).

FRAME MENU, Frame typography   MENU COMMANDS

The Frame Typography dialog box appears (see Figure 5–44.) Operation of the features in this dialog box is identical to the operation of the **Chapter Typography** dialog box (Chapter menu). Selecting **Default** sets that feature to the value provided in the Chapter Typography option. Selecting any other setting overrides the Chapter Typography for this frame.

REFERENCE GUIDE   5-109

Figure 12.2 (continued).

Anchors & caption settings

```
┌─────────────────────────────────────────────┐
│ ANCHORS & CAPTIONS                        [?] │
│   Anchor:  Nozzle_____                     │
│  Caption:  Below    ↕                         │
│    Label:  Figure [C#]·[F#]|_____        │
│  Inserts:  [Table #] [Figure #] [Chapter #] [Text Attr.] │
│                              [ OK ]  [Cancel] │
└─────────────────────────────────────────────┘
```

Figure 5–45   Anchors & Caption Setting dialog box

Description

The **Anchors & Caption Settings** option allows you to:

- Assign an anchor name to a frame.
- Attach a caption frame above, below, or to the left or right of any given frame.

Two different caption counters—a Table counter and a Figure counter—can be used to number captions. These counters are automatically updated as you add and delete captions. (See the **Update Counters** option in the Chapter menu.)

All captions for a chapter are stored in a caption file. You can edit and check this file for spelling errors later using the ASCII text function of a standard word processor.

Application

- Create captions for pictures
- Automatically generate figure/table numbers
- Anchor a picture to a location in the text

Figure 12.2 (continued).

Figure 12.3 shows a selection from the *Microsoft Macro Assembler 5.1 Programmer's Guide*, a reference manual that is arranged by task, somewhat like a procedures guide. The sample pages are from a section in Chapter 11 called "Using Macros," which is organized into task-oriented groups as follows:

> Using Macros
> > Defining Macros
> > Calling Macros
> > Using Local Symbols
> > Exiting from a Macro

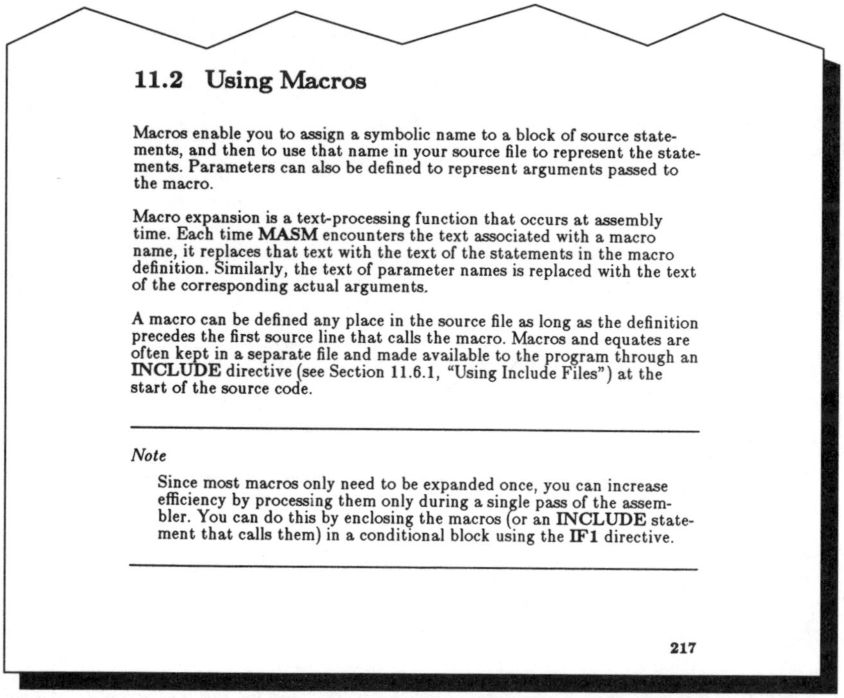

11.2   Using Macros

Macros enable you to assign a symbolic name to a block of source statements, and then to use that name in your source file to represent the statements. Parameters can also be defined to represent arguments passed to the macro.

Macro expansion is a text-processing function that occurs at assembly time. Each time **MASM** encounters the text associated with a macro name, it replaces that text with the text of the statements in the macro definition. Similarly, the text of parameter names is replaced with the text of the corresponding actual arguments.

A macro can be defined any place in the source file as long as the definition precedes the first source line that calls the macro. Macros and equates are often kept in a separate file and made available to the program through an **INCLUDE** directive (see Section 11.6.1, "Using Include Files") at the start of the source code.

Note

Since most macros only need to be expanded once, you can increase efficiency by processing them only during a single pass of the assembler. You can do this by enclosing the macros (or an **INCLUDE** statement that calls them) in a conditional block using the **IF1** directive.

217

Figure 12.3. Pages from a Command Reference Section Organized by Task (from *Microsoft Macro Assembler 5.1 Programmer's Guide*). Note that the basic structure of each module is introduction, syntax, details about options, example.

Often a task can be done by using either a macro or procedure. For example, the addup procedure shown in Section 17.4.3, "Passing Arguments on the Stack," does the same thing as the addup macro in Section 11.2.1, "Defining Macros." Macros are expanded on every occurrence of the macro name, so they can increase the length of the executable file if called repeatedly. Procedures are coded only once in the executable file, but the increased overhead of saving and restoring addresses and parameters can make them slower.

The section below tells how to define and call macros. Repeat blocks, a special form of macro for doing repeated operations, are discussed separately in Section 11.3.

11.2.1   Defining Macros

The **MACRO** and **ENDM** directives are used to define macros. **MACRO** designates the beginning of the macro block and **ENDM** designates the end of the macro block.

■   **Syntax**

name   **MACRO** [*parameter* [*,parameter*]...]
statements
ENDM

The *name* must be unique and a valid symbol name. It can be used later in the source file to invoke the macro.

The *parameters* (sometimes called dummy parameters) are names that act as placeholders for values to be passed as arguments to the macro when it is called. Any number of *parameters* can be specified, but they must all fit on one line. If you give more than one parameter, you must separate them with commas, spaces, or tabs. Commas can always be used as separators; spaces and tabs may cause ambiguity if the arguments are expressions.

Note

This manual uses the term "parameter" to refer to a placeholder for a value that will be passed to a macro or procedure. Parameters appear in macro or procedure definitions. The term "argument" is used to refer to an actual value passed to the macro or procedure when it is called.

Any valid assembler statement may be placed within a macro, including statements that call or define other macros. Any number of statements can

218

Figure 12.3   (continued).

be used. The *parameters* can be used any number of times in the statements. Macros can be nested, redefined, or used recursively, as explained in Section 11.5, "Using Recursive, Nested, and Redefined Macros."

MASM assembles the statements in a macro only if the macro is called, and only at the point in the source file from which it is called. The macro definition itself is never assembled.

A macro definition can include the **LOCAL** directive, which lets you define labels used only within a macro, or the **EXITM** directive, which allows you to exit from a macro before all the statements in the block are expanded. These directives are discussed in Sections 11.2.3, "Using Local Symbols," and 11.2.4, "Exiting from a Macro." Macro operators can also be used in macro definitions, as described in Section 11.4, "Using Macro Operators."

■ **Example**

```
addup      MACRO    ad1,ad2,ad3
           mov      ax,ad1      ;; First parameter in AX
           add      ax,ad2      ;; Add next two parameters
           add      ax,ad3      ;;   and leave sum in AX
           ENDM
```

The preceding example defines a macro named addup, which uses three parameters to add three values and leave their sum in the **AX** register. The three parameters will be replaced with arguments when the macro is called.

11.2.2 Calling Macros

A macro call directs **MASM** to copy the statements of the macro to the point of the call and to replace any parameters in the macro statements with the corresponding actual arguments.

■ **Syntax**

name [argument [,argument]...]

The *name* must be the name of a macro defined earlier in the source file. The *arguments* can be any text. For example, symbols, constants, and registers are often given as arguments. Any number of arguments can be given, but they must all fit on one line. Multiple arguments must be separated by commas, spaces, or tabs.

MASM replaces the first parameter with the first argument, the second parameter with the second argument, and so on. If a macro call has more

Figure 12.3 (continued).

arguments than the macro has parameters, the extra arguments are ignored. If a call has fewer arguments than the macro has parameters, any remaining parameters are replaced with a null (empty) string.

You can use conditional statements to enable macros to check for null strings or other types of arguments. The macro can then take appropriate action to adjust to different kinds of arguments. See Chapter 10, "Assembling Conditionally," for more information on using conditional-assembly and conditional-error directives to test macro arguments.

■ **Example**

```
addup     MACRO    ad1,ad2,ad3        ; Macro definition
          mov      ax,ad1             ;; First parameter in AX
          add      ax,ad2             ;; Add next two parameters
          add      ax,ad3             ;;   and leave sum in AX
          ENDM
          .
          .
          .
          addup    bx,2,count         ; Macro call
```

When the addup macro is called, **MASM** replaces the parameters with the actual parameters given in the macro call. In the example above, the assembler would expand the macro call to the following code:

```
          mov      ax,bx
          add      ax,2
          add      ax,count
```

This code could be shown in an assembler listing, depending on whether the **.LALL**, **.XALL**, or **.SALL** directive was in effect (see Section 12.3.3, "Controlling Listing of Macros").

11.2.3 Using Local Symbols

The **LOCAL** directive can be used within a macro to define symbols that are available only within the defined macro.

Note

In this context, the term "local" is not related to the public availability of a symbol, as described in Chapter 8, "Creating Programs from Multiple Modules," or to variables that are defined to be local to a procedure, as described in Section 17.4.4, "Using Local Variables." "Local" simply means that the symbol is not known outside the macro where it is defined.

Figure 12.3 (continued).

■ **Syntax**

LOCAL *localname* [*,localname*]...

The *localname* is a temporary symbol name that is to be replaced by a unique symbol name when the macro is expanded. At least cne *localname* is required for each **LOCAL** directive. If more than one local symbol is given, the names must be separated with commas. Once declared, *localname* can be used in any statement within the macro definition.

MASM creates a new actual name for *localname* each time the macro is expanded. The actual name has the following form:

??number

The *number* is a hexadecimal number in the range 0000 to 0FFFF. You should not give other symbols names in this format, since doing so may produce a symbol with multiple definitions. In listings, the local name is shown in the macro definition, but the actual name is shown in expansions of macro calls.

Nonlocal labels may be used in a macro; but if the macro is used more than once, the same label will appear in both expansions, and **MASM** will display an error message, indicating that the file contains a symbol with multiple definitions. To avoid this problem, use only local labels (or redefinable equates) in macros.

Note

> The **LOCAL** directive can only be used in macro definitions, and it must precede all other statements in the definition. If you try another statement (such as a comment instruction) before the **LOCAL** directive, an error will be generated.

■ **Example**

```
power      MACRO    factor,exponent    ;; Use for unsigned only
           LOCAL    again,gotzero      ;; Declare symbols for macro
           xor      dx,dx              ;; Clear DX
           mov      cx,exponent        ;; Exponent is count for loop
           mov      ax,1               ;; Multiply by 1 first time
           jcxz     gotzero            ;; Get out if exponent is zero
           mov      bx,factor
again:     mul      bx                 ;; Multiply until done
           loop     again
gotzero:
           ENDM
```

Figure 12.3 (continued).

Figure 12.4 shows two sample pages from the *DataViz MacLinkPlus Reference Guide*. These are good examples of reference pages describing a screen.

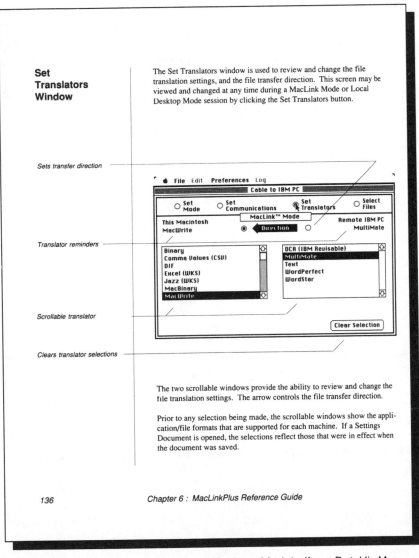

Figure 12.4. Pages from a Screen Reference Module (from *DataViz Mac-LinkPlus Reference Guide*).

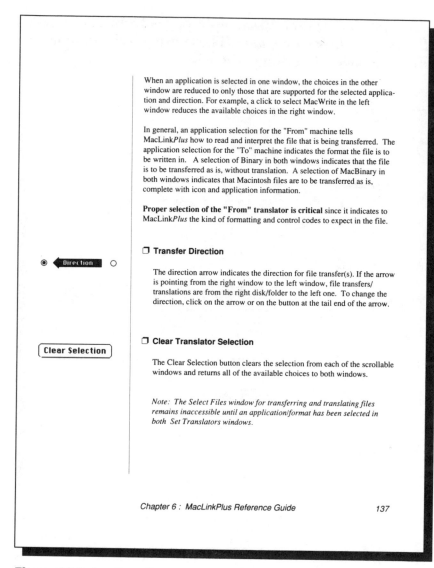

When an application is selected in one window, the choices in the other window are reduced to only those that are supported for the selected application and direction. For example, a click to select MacWrite in the left window reduces the available choices in the right window.

In general, an application selection for the "From" machine tells MacLink*Plus* how to read and interpret the file that is being transferred. The application selection for the "To" machine indicates the format the file is to be written in. A selection of Binary in both windows indicates that the file is to be transferred as is, without translation. A selection of MacBinary in both windows indicates that Macintosh files are to be transferred as is, complete with icon and application information.

Proper selection of the "From" translator is critical since it indicates to MacLink*Plus* the kind of formatting and control codes to expect in the file.

❏ Transfer Direction

The direction arrow indicates the direction for file transfer(s). If the arrow is pointing from the right window to the left window, file transfers/translations are from the right disk/folder to the left one. To change the direction, click on the arrow or on the button at the tail end of the arrow.

❏ Clear Translator Selection

The Clear Selection button clears the selection from each of the scrollable windows and returns all of the available choices to both windows.

Note: The Select Files window for transferring and translating files remains inaccessible until an application/format has been selected in both Set Translators windows.

Chapter 6 : MacLinkPlus Reference Guide   137

Figure 12.4 (continued).

Figure 12.5 shows a sample page from the message reference section of the *Microsoft Macro Assembler 5.1 Programmer's Guide*.

Error Messages and Exit Codes

Code	Message
0	Block nesting error

Nested procedures, segments, structures, macros, or repeat blocks were not properly terminated. This error may indicate that you closed an outer level of nesting with inner levels still open.

| 1 | Extra characters on line |

Sufficient information to define a statement has been received on a line, but additional characters were also provided. This may indicate that you provided too many arguments.

| 2 | Internal error - Register already defined *symbol* |

Note the conditions when the error occurs and contact Microsoft Corporation by using the Product Assistance Request form at the end of this manual.

| 3 | Unknown type specifier |

An invalid type specifier was used to give the size of a label or external declaration. For instance, **BYTE** or **NEAR** might have been misspelled.

| 4 | Redefinition of symbol |

A symbol was defined in two places with different types. This error occurs during Pass 1 on the second declaration of the symbol.

| 5 | Symbol is multidefined: |

A symbol is defined in two places. This error occurs during Pass 2 on each declaration of the symbol.

| 6 | Phase error between passes |

An ambiguous instruction or directive caused the relative address of a label to be changed between Pass 1 and Pass 2. You can use the /D option to produce a Pass 1 listing to aid in resolving phase errors between passes. The format of Pass 1 listings is discussed in Section 2.5.7.

| 7 | Already had ELSE clause |

More than one **ELSE** clause was used within a conditional assembly block. Each nested **ELSE** must have its own **IF** directive and **ENDIF**.

431

Figure 12.5. Page from a Message Reference Section (from *Microsoft Macro Assembler 5.1 Programmer's Guide*).

CHAPTER 13

Organizing Quick Reference Pieces

A quick reference piece can be one of the following:

- quick reference card (one piece, usually printed on both sides)

- quick reference guide (small booklet)

- keyboard template (printed cutout that fits around or is affixed to a keyboard)

Quick reference pieces list important keys, commands, or functions. They normally don't include procedures (at least not more than one or two), definitions, descriptions of results, or conditions for use. If a program employs several different screens, a quick reference piece may include pictures of the screens with callouts to important details, such as icons, message lines, parts of the screen you can click on, and so forth. When you develop quick reference materials, you assume that users know how to use the program but may need to be reminded of a command or key combination. You can print quick reference information on the inside cover of a manual or on a separate, perforated page that can easily be removed.

Because quick reference cards or guides help intermediate and expert users find the command or key they need without having to thumb through many pages of descriptive text, they are always welcome additions to a software manual.

While they are learning the program, novice users are always glad to have keyboard templates, which fit on top of a keyboard. However, most experienced users find them a nuisance, especially if they use a variety of programs on a daily basis. After all, keyboards don't have room to attach more than one keyboard template at a time, and they can get in the way of typing.

GUIDELINES FOR QUICK REFERENCE PIECES

The key word in a quick reference piece is "quick." Don't include any text—such as descriptions, explanations, or procedures—that can't be read at a glance. Include only lists of commands, options, or keys.

If you're going to create keyboard templates, make sure the key descriptions will appear next to the keys they reference. Also, keep in mind that not all keyboards are alike, so if your program runs on a variety of equipment, you may need to develop more than one keyboard template.

SAMPLE QUICK REFERENCE PIECES

The first quick reference piece we'll show here is the *Lotus 1-2-3®* *Quick Reference Guide* (a small booklet) from the version 2.0 package. In Figure 13.1, which is an excerpt of several pages, you'll see that the *Quick Reference Guide* consists of lists of the program's functions, macros, keys, filenames, labels, and operators, arranged according to the following outline:

Functions
    Mathematical Functions
    Logical Functions
    Special Functions
    String Functions
    Date and Time Functions
    Financial Functions
    Statistical Functions
    Database Statistical Functions

Macros
    Summary of Macro Names for Special Keys
    Macro Command Keyword Summary
    The /X Macro Commands

Names for Keys
    Standard Keys
    Pointer-Movement Keys
    Combination Pointer-Movement Keys

1-2-3 File Names

Label Alignments

Arithmetic and Logical Operators

@Functions

@ABS *(x)*
Absolute, or positive, value of *x*

Mathematical
@Functions

@ACOS *(x)*
Arc cosine of *x*

@ASIN *(x)*
Arc sine of *x*

@ATAN *(x)*
2-quadrant arc tangent of *x*

@ATAN2 *(x,y)*
4-quadrant arc tangent of *y/x*

@COS *(x)*
Cosine of angle *x*

@EXP *(x)*
The number *e* (2.71828...) raised to the *x*th power

@INT *(x)*
Integer part of *x*

@LN *(x)*
Natural log (base *e*) of *x*

@LOG *(x)*
Log (base 10) of *x*

@MOD *(x/y)*
Remainder of *x/y*

@PI
The number π (3.1415926...)

@RAND
Random number between 0 and 1

@ROUND *(x,n)*
x rounded to *n* places

@SIN *(x)*
Sine of angle *x*

@SQRT *(x)*
Positive square root of *x*

@TAN *(x)*
Tangent of angle *x*

Logical Functions

@FALSE
Logical value 0 (FALSE)

2

Figure 13.1. Pages from a Quick Reference Guide (from *Lotus 1-2-3®*
Quick Reference Guide).

Statistical Functions

@AVG *(list)*
Average of the values in *list*

@COUNT *(list)*
Number of non-blank entries in *list*

@MAX *(list)*
Maximum value in *list*

@MIN *(list)*
Minimum value in *list*

@STD *(list)*
Population standard deviation of the values in *list*

@SUM *(list)*
Sum of the values in *list*

@VAR *(list)*
Population variance of the values in *list*

Database Statistical Functions

@DAVG *(input, offset, criterion)*
Average of the values in the *offset* column of the *input* range that meet the criteria in the *criterion* range

@DCOUNT *(input, offset, criterion)*
Number of non-blank cells in the *offset* column of the *input* range that meet the criteria in the *criterion* range

@DMAX *(input, offset, criterion)*
Maximum value in the *offset* column of the *input* range that meets the criteria in the *criterion* range

@DMIN *(input, offset, criterion)*
Minimum value in the *offset* column of the *input* range that meets the criteria in the *criterion* range

@DSTD *(input, offset, criterion)*
Population standard deviation of the values in the *offset* column of the *input* range that meet the criteria in the *criterion* range

@DSUM *(input, offset, criterion)*
Sum of the values in the *offset* column of the *input* range that meet the criteria in the *criterion* range

@DVAR *(input, offset, criterion)*
Population variance for values in the *offset* column of the *input* range that meet the criteria in the *criterion* range

7

Figure 13.1 (continued).

Macros	{abs}	{escape} or {esc} {right}
	{backspace} or {bs}	{goto} {table}
Summary of Macro	{bigleft}	{graph} {up}
Names for Special Keys	{bigright}	{home} {window}
	{calc}	{left}
	{delete} or {del}	{name} ˜(the RETURN key)
	{down}	{pgdn} {˜} (Tilde)
	{edit}	{pgup} {{} (Left brace)
	{end}	{query} {}} (Right brace)

**Macro Command
Keyword Summary**

Note: Arguments in < > are optional.

{?}
Halts macro execution temporarily for keyboard input.

{**routine-name** <optional-argument>, <optional-argument>...}
Calls a subroutine.

{**BEEP** <number>}
Sounds the computer's bell or tone.

{**BLANK** *location*}
Erases the contents of a specified cell or range.

{**BRANCH** *location*}
Continues executing macro instructions located in a different cell.

{**BREAKOFF**}
Disables the BREAK key during macro execution.

{**BREAKON**}
Restores the BREAK key, undoing {BREAKOFF}.

{**CLOSE**}
Closes a file that has been opened with the {OPEN} command.

{**CONTENTS** *destination-location,source-location*,
<width-number>,<format-number>}
Places the contents of one cell in another cell as a label.

{**DEFINE** *location1:type1,location2:type2,...*}
Specifies cells that store arguments in a subroutine call.

{**DISPATCH** *location*}
Branches indirectly to specified destination.

8

Figure 13.1 (continued).

**The /X Macro
Commands**

/XClocation ~
Instructs 1-2-3 to go to a specified location and to continue reading
macro instructions at that location until it encounters an /XR
command.

/XGlocation ~
Instructs 1-2-3 to read the keystroke instructions at a specified
location.

/XIcondition ~...
An if-then-else statement that tests the result of a specified
condition.

/XLmessage ~ *location* ~
Displays a message on the control panel and waits for you to enter
any characters placed in the specified location.

/XMlocation ~
Allows you to construct a customized menu (up to eight choices).

/XNmessage ~ *location* ~
Displays a message on the control panel and waits for you to enter
any number or formula (including range names and @functions)
placed in the specified location.

/XQ
Stops macro execution.

/XR
Instructs 1-2-3 to return to main macro routine to continue reading
keystroke instructions immediately following the /XClocation ~
command.

11

Figure 13.1 (continued).

Names for Keys

Standard Keys

Name	Definition
ABS	Cycles a cell address through relative, absolute, and mixed in POINT and EDIT modes.
BACKSPACE	Erases character to left of cursor; if a range is selected, erases current range.
BACKTAB	In READY mode, moves cell pointer one screen to the left; in EDIT mode, moves cursor five characters to the left.
BREAK	Cancels current operation.
CALC	Recalculates worksheet formulas in READY mode; converts a formula into its current value in VALUE and EDIT modes.
CAPS LOCK	When pressed, switches between uppercase and lower-case letters. Number and punctuation keys are not affected.
COMPOSE	When used in combination with certain keys, creates international characters.
CONTROL	When used in combination with certain keys, changes the function of those keys.
DELETE	Erases current character in EDIT mode.
EDIT	Places highlighted entry on the control panel for editing.
ESCAPE	Cancels current entry or range, or returns to previous command step.
GOTO	Moves cell pointer to the cell you specify.
GRAPH	Displays the graph most recently specified.
HELP	Invokes the Help facility.
INSERT	Switches between inserting text by moving existing text to the right, and replacing existing text in EDIT mode.
MACRO	Invokes a macro when used in combination with a macro name.
NAME	Displays menu of the current range names in POINT mode and in conjunction with GOTO.
PERIOD	Makes the current cell the anchor cell when the range is unanchored, or cycles the anchor cell and the free cell in range.
QUERY	Repeats most recent /Data Query procedure.
RETURN	Completes an entry, a command, or part of a command.

(Continued)

12

Figure 13.1 (continued).

Name	Definition
SCROLL LOCK	Switches arrow keys between moving the pointer and moving the window.
SHIFT	When used in combination with another key on the typewriter section of keyboard, produces the upper symbol on the key.
SPACE	Inserts a space.
STEP	Allows you to move through a macro, step by step.
TAB	In READY mode, moves pointer one screen to the right; in EDIT mode, moves cursor five characters to the right.
TABLE	Repeats most recent /Data Table procedure.
WINDOW	Switches pointer between the two windows when there is a split screen.

Pointer-Movement Keys

Name	Definition
DOWN	In READY and POINT modes, moves cell pointer down one cell; in HELP mode, down one item; in EDIT mode, completes entry and moves cell pointer down one cell.
END	In READY and POINT modes, must be used with another pointer-movement key. In MENU and HELP modes, moves cell pointer to last item; in EDIT mode, to last character.
HOME	In READY and POINT modes, moves cell pointer to upper left corner; in MENU and HELP modes, to first item; in EDIT mode, to first character.
LEFT	In READY and POINT modes, moves cell pointer left one cell; in MENU and HELP modes, left one item; in EDIT mode, left one character.
PAGE DOWN	In READY and POINT modes, moves cell pointer down one page; in EDIT mode, completes entry and moves cell pointer down one screen.
PAGE UP	In READY and POINT modes, moves cell pointer up one page; in EDIT mode, completes entry and moves cell pointer up one screen.
RIGHT	In READY and POINT modes, moves cell pointer right one cell; in MENU and HELP modes, right one item; in EDIT mode, right one character.
UP	In READY and POINT modes, moves cell pointer up one cell; in HELP mode, up one item; in EDIT mode, completes entry and moves cell pointer up one cell.

13

Figure 13.1 (continued).

Combination Pointer-Movement Keys	Name	Definition
	BIG LEFT	In READY and POINT modes, left one screen. In EDIT mode, left five characters.
	BIG RIGHT	In READY and POINT modes, right one page. In EDIT mode, right five characters.
	END DOWN	In READY and POINT modes, down to next intersection of blank and filled cell.
	END HOME	In READY and POINT modes, lower right corner of active area.
	END LEFT	In READY and POINT modes, left to next intersection of blank and filled cell.
	END RIGHT	In READY and POINT modes, right to next intersection of blank and filled cell.
	END UP	In READY and POINT modes, up to next intersection of blank and filled cell.

1-2-3 File Names

File names can be up to eight characters long, and include upper-case and lowercase letters, numbers, and the underscore (_) character. Check your operating system manual to see if it will accept any other special characters.

1-2-3 automatically adds an extension appropriate to the type of file you are naming:

.WK1   worksheet file

.PRN   print (text) file

.PIC   graph (picture) file

.CTF   character code translation file

(Driver sets that you create with the Install program automatically receive the extension .SET.)

When you specify a file that is not stored in the current directory or drive, precede the file name with a drive specifier and/or a pathname of subdirectories. For example:

B:\SALESFIG
C:\NEWACCTS\ACCT3.WK1

14

Figure 13.1 (continued).

Label Alignments

Label-prefix characters determine how a label is aligned in a cell. You cannot assign a label prefix to a cell itself, only to its label entry.

Label Prefix	Alignment
' (apostrophe)	Left
" (double-quote)	Right
^ (caret)	Center
\ (backslash)	Repeating

/Worksheet Global Label-Prefix: Sets global label prefix, which 1-2-3 automatically adds to any label entered without a prefix.

/Range Label: Changes the label prefix for all labels in a range.

Long Labels: 240 characters; maximum character length in a cell.

Arithmetic and Logical Operators

Operator	Precedence Meaning	Precedence Number
^	Exponentiation	7 (highest)
+	Positive	6
–	Negative	6
*	Multiplication	5
/	Division	5
+	Addition	4
–	Subtraction	4
=	Equal	3
<	Less than	3
< =	Less than or equal	3
>	Greater than	3
> =	Greater than or equal	3
< >	Not equal	3
#NOT#	Logical NOT	2
#AND#	Logical AND	1
#OR#	Logical OR	1
&	String combination	1 (lowest)

15

Figure 13.1 (continued).

Figure 13.2 shows the *Samna Amí Quick Reference Card*. This card is a 8½ by 14½ inch piece of stiff paper, printed and folded in half to appear as four different panels.

Figure 13.2 shows that this quick reference card consists of lists of icon, keyboard, and mouse shortcuts, followed by lists of keys used to choose commands and options (Working with Amí) and keys used to move the cursor (Working with Text).

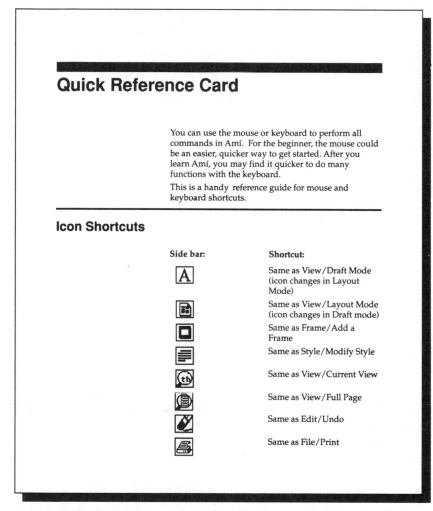

Figure 13.2. Panels of a Quick Reference Card (from *Samna Amí Quick Reference Card*).

Quick Reference Card

Keyboard Shortcuts

Some of the more frequently used commands have control key-based shortcuts.

Note: Many of these shortcuts are shown on the screen next to the appropriate menu item. In the menus, ^ indicates to press and hold [CTRL].

Command:	Shortcut:
Align Center	CTRL + C
Align Left	CTRL + L
Align Right	CTRL + R
Bold	CTRL + B
Copy	CTRL + Insert
Cut	SHIFT + DEL
Draft/Layout Mode	CTRL + M
Full Page/Current View	CTRL + V
Go To	CTRL + G
Italic	CTRL + I
Justify	CTRL + J
Modify Style	CTRL + A
Normal	CTRL + N
Paste	Shift + Insert
Print	CTRL + P
Save	CTRL + S
Select A Style	CTRL + Y
Select Next Frame	CTRL + F
Show/Hide Side Bar	CTRL + Q
Show/Hide Styles Box	CTRL + Z

Figure 13.2 (continued).

Quick Reference Card

| Underline | CTRL + U |
| Undo | ALT + BkSp |

Mouse Shortcuts

Go To	Double click on the Page Number box
Modify Style	Double click on the current style indicator in the Styles Box
Select a Word	Double click on the word
	Dragging the mouse over the word
Open a document	Double click on the document's name

Working with Amí

Selecting menus, commands, and the options from the keyboard:

To:	**Press:**
Select a menu	ALT + the underlined letter of the menu name
Select a command	ALT + the first letter of the menu name + the underlined letter in the command name
Move to the next group of options	Tab

Figure 13.2 (continued).

Quick Reference Card

Move up or down through a group of option buttons or check boxes	Up or Down arrow
Choose the command with the selected command button	Return
Cancel the dialog box	Escape

Working with Text

Moving the text cursor and adjusting the text selection:

To move the cursor:	Press:
To beginning of line	Home
To end of line	End
Left one character	Left arrow
Right one character	Right arrow
Left one word	CTRL + Left arrow
Right one word	CTRL + Right arrow
Up one line	Up arrow
Down one line	Down arrow
Up one screen	CTRL + Page Up
Down one screen	CTRL + Page Down
To start of document	CTRL + Home
To end of document	CTRL + End

Figure 13.2 (continued).

CHAPTER 14

On-line Help and Screen Messages

There's a growing trend toward putting documentation on computer disks rather than on paper. The reasons behind this trend are

○ on-line documentation is frequently cheaper to produce than printed manuals

○ modern computers have sufficient memory to store and sort through large amounts of text easily

○ on-line documentation keeps the users' attention on the computer screen, while printed documentation pulls it away

DIFFERENCES BETWEEN PRINTED AND ON-LINE DOCUMENTATION

Unfortunately, you can't just take your old software manuals and display the pages on the monitor screen to create on-line documentation. On-line documentation requires different techniques.

Why? For one thing, text displayed on a monitor screen can't be read as quickly or understood as easily as printed text. Because of the differences in resolution, in letter shapes, in line and character spacing, and in contrast with the background, it simply lacks the legibility of printed text.

For another thing, users can get lost in extensive on-line documentation. We're all familiar with books: we can see where they begin and end, and we can see the relationship of each page to the rest of the book. But users can't easily see the relationship of a screenful of information to the rest of the system. So you need to provide more "road signs" to help users find their way around.

Many software programs now include two forms of on-line documentation: on-line help systems and collections of messages that appear on the screen to guide users. Although the implementation of help systems and screen messages is considered a programming task, the documentation writer should either write the text for them or at least review it to make sure the wording and style is consistent with the printed documentation. Otherwise, different terms and conflicting procedures may confuse users.

GUIDELINES FOR SCREEN MESSAGES

If you're writing or reviewing messages that will appear on the screen, follow these guidelines:

○ Messages should be consistent in terminology and style with other pieces in the documentation package.

○ Messages should be meaningful to users and, whenever possible, should guide them to the correct action. For example, *Spaces not allowed in filename* is much more helpful than *Bad filename* or *Illegal error 102*.

GUIDELINES FOR HELP SYSTEMS

On-line help systems run the gamut from very simple to very sophisticated, so it's difficult to develop hard-and-fast rules for them. Here are some general guidelines for every help system:

○ Let users control when to display a new screenful of information and when to exit.

○ Divide the information into screenfuls of text in which the text takes up no more than 25 percent of the screen.

○ Put "road signs" on each screen in the form of subject titles and screen numbers (if there's more than one screenful of information about that subject). For example, if a section of your help system tells how to use the OPEN FILE command

and there are two screens of information about it, you might want to title the first one OPEN FILE COMMAND—SCREEN 1 of 2 so users will know exactly what they're reading and that there's another screen to come.

○ If your help information is complex, create layers with general information on top and details on the bottom.

○ If at all possible, display the help information in a separate window or split the screen so that users can see both the program and the help information at once.

BASIC ORGANIZATIONS FOR HELP SYSTEMS

You can create a simple on-line help system by dividing the information contained in your quick reference materials into help screens. Of course, you've got to come up with methods to let users know just what information the help system contains (some kind of menu) and then how to display the information they need (some way to jump to a specific screen).

To make an on-line help system more helpful, you may want to do one of the following:

○ Give users the ability to search for specific text.

○ Make the help system "context sensitive" by linking commands or screen areas (such as fill-in fields) to appropriate sections of help information. Then, when the focus is on one of the linked commands or areas and the user asks for help, the appropriate information is automatically displayed.

A sophisticated help system might also allow users to

○ mark a location in the help information and "jump" to that marked location (sometimes referred to as *bookmarking*)

○ add their own information to the help system

○ print information from the help system

Many help systems also include an "About" screen, which states the name and version number of the program, the name of the company or group that produced it, and sometimes a phone number users can call to get more information.

SAMPLE ON-LINE HELP SYSTEMS

In this section, you'll see screen shots of on-line help systems from several retail software packages.

A SIMPLE HELP SYSTEM

This section shows screen shots from the help system included with *DOS Quick Reference*, a part of the *Microsoft Learning DOS* tutorial package.

Figure 14.1 shows the main screen for the *Microsoft DOS Quick Reference*, and Figure 14.2 shows a help screen.

```
Microsoft (c) 1986-88      DOS Quick Reference Index        Page 1 of 3

INTERNAL DOS COMMANDS

   cd (chdir)      date         fastopen      rd (rmdir)    ver
   chcp            del          fdisk         rename        verify
   cls             dir          md (mkdir)    set           vol
   copy            erase        path          time
   ctty            exit         prompt        type


EXTERNAL DOS COMMANDS

   append          debug        graftabl      nlsfunc       sort
   assign          diskcomp     graphics      print         subst
   attrib          diskcopy     join          recover       sys
   backup          edlin        keyb          replace       tree
   chkdsk          exe2bin      label         restore       xcopy
   command         find         mode          select        fc (MS-DOS
   comp            format       more          share             only)

 Press PgDn for more commands      Press Esc to use DOS
 Press ? to get help               Enter a command or topic ▸ _
```

Figure 14.1. Access to an On-line Help System (from *Microsoft DOS Quick Reference*). This screen is from the main program. Note how the message in the lower left corner tells users how they can get help: *Press ? to get help*.

```
Microsoft (c) 1986-88      DOS Quick Reference -- help        Page 1 of 4

How to Use DOS Quick Reference

   To get help on a command or topic, type the command and press Enter
   when you see this prompt:   Enter a command or topic ▸

Keys you can use:

    PgUp  or  PgDn      To move from page to page and topic to topic.
                        You can use PgDn to see every page of DOS Quick
                        Reference.  When you get to the end, you will
                        return to the Index.

    Enter               To see the Index.

    Esc                 To leave DOS Quick Reference and use DOS.

DOS command notation:
   See pages 3 and 4 to learn how to read DOS commands.


 Press PgDn for more help          Press Esc to use DOS
 Press PgUp to continue            Press Enter to see Index
```

Figure 14.2. A Simple On-line Help System (from *Microsoft DOS Quick Reference*). Note that users can tell exactly where they are in the system: all the "road signs" they need are at the top of each screen.

```
Microsoft (c) 1986-88     DOS Quick Reference -- help          Page 2 of 4

Shortcuts You Can Use

Entering command and topic names:

   You only need to enter enough of a command to distinguish it from
   other commands.  For example, entering  er  will give you information
   on the Erase command.  If you don't enter enough of the command's or
   topic's name, you will get a message telling you to check the Index.

Going directly to a command from DOS:

   You can get help on a command or topic from DOS without going through
   the DOS Quick Reference Index.  Enter  help command  at the DOS
   prompt.  Example:  help backup


DOS command notation:
   See the next two pages to learn how to read DOS commands.


   Press PgDn for more help        Press Esc to use DOS
   Press PgUp for Page 1           Press Enter to see Index
```

Figure 14.2 (continued). Keys that control the Help display are clearly explained at the bottom of each screen.

```
Microsoft (c) 1986-88     DOS Quick Reference -- help          Page 3 of 4

How to read the DOS commands.

                         command   [<drive:>]   <filename>

 ■ The DOS command. ────────────┘      ↑    ↑    ↑    ↑

 ■ The square brackets [] mean this
   is an optional parameter.  Don't ──────────┘    │
   enter the brackets.

 ■ The angle brackets <> mean that you
   substitute information for the word in ───────────┘
   brackets.  Don't enter the brackets.

   In these examples, you would have to enter the command
   and the filename, but the drive would be optional.
   Examples:  type plan.doc  OR  type a:plan.doc


   Press PgDn for more help        Press Esc to use DOS
   Press PgUp for Page 2           Press Enter to see Index
```

Figure 14.2 (continued).

```
Microsoft (c) 1986-88     DOS Quick Reference -- help          Page 4 of 4

You substitute command information for words in angle brackets.
Don't enter the brackets.

   <drive:>      A drive name. (Examples:  a:  b:  c:)

  <filename>     The name of a file including the extension if any.
                 (Examples:  budget.mp  plan.doc)

  <pathname>     The name of a file including any directory names that DOS
                 needs to locate the file.
                 (Example:  \midwest\sales\jansales.mp)

   <path>        The name of a directory including any other directory names
                 that DOS needs to locate the directory.
                 (Example:  \budgets\midwest\sales)

  Switches       Modify DOS commands.  Switches begin with a slash /
                 (Examples:  /a  /f  /d:<date>)


 Press PgDn to continue          Press Esc to use DOS
 Press PgUp for Page 3           Press Enter to see Index
```

Figure 14.2 (continued).

A SOPHISTICATED HELP SYSTEM

Figures 14.3 and 14.4 show sample screens that represent a small portion of the *Apple HyperCard* help system.

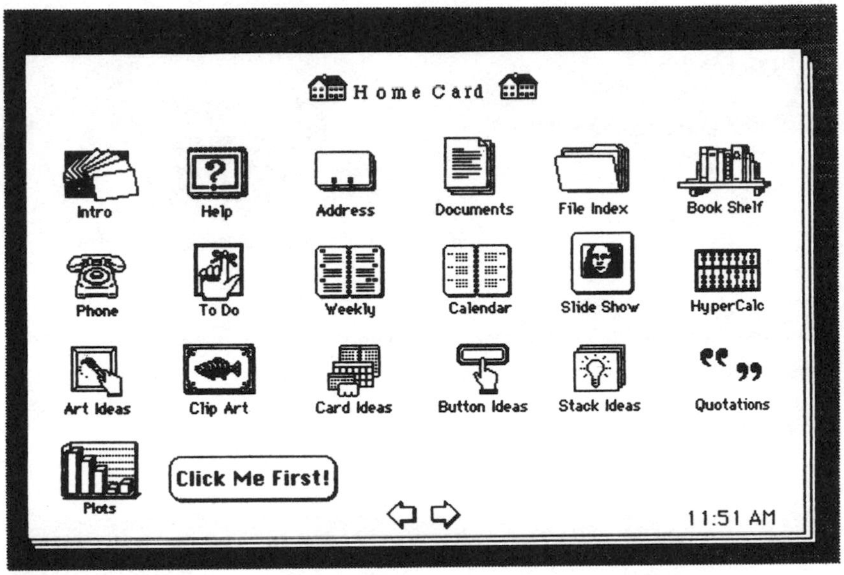

Figure 14.3. Access to an On-line Help System (from *Apple HyperCard*). Users can get help from the HyperCard Home Card (the main screen) by clicking on the Help icon in the first row of icons.

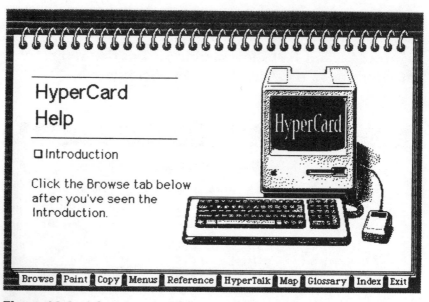

Figure 14.4. A Sophisticated Help System (from *Apple HyperCard*). On this introductory screen, users can click on the square Introduction "button" to see the rest of the screens in the Help Introduction.

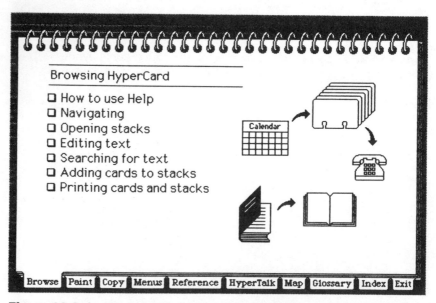

Figure 14.4 (continued). This is one of the many main topic screens in the HyperCard Help system. Users can quickly tell where they are by looking at the "tabs" at the bottom of the screen. To navigate through the Help system, users click on the tab labeled with the topic they want to see. Clicking on the last tab, Exit, takes users back to the main screen, the Home Card.

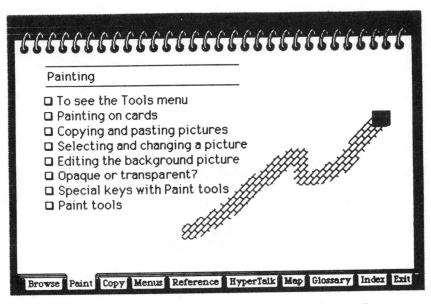

Figure 14.4 (continued). Users can click on the buttons (the small shadowed squares, arrows, and other icons) on the main topic screens to see subtopics with additional explanations.

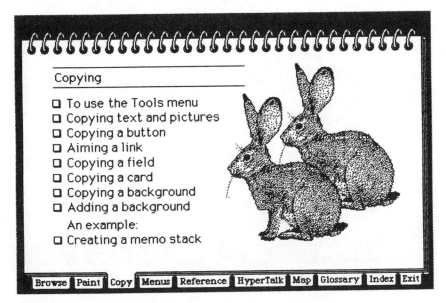

Figure 14.4 (continued).

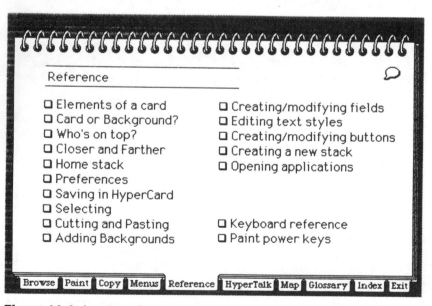

Figure 14.4 (continued).

Figure 14.4 (continued).

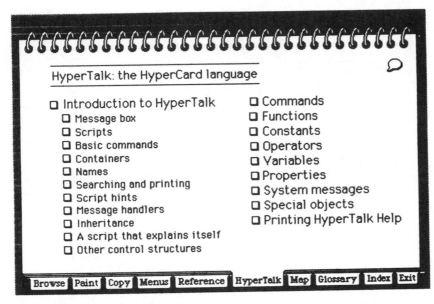

Figure 14.4 (continued).

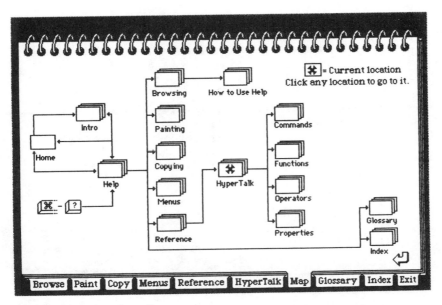

Figure 14.4 (continued).

Figure 14.4 (continued).

Figure 14.4 (continued).

APPLYING WRITING TECHNIQUES

Writing is a skill with basic and advanced techniques, just like drafting, accounting, or programming. Most of us learned the basics of composition while we were in school. For some, writing is intuitive and easy; for others, it's a tedious chore.

The writing techniques described in this part of the book are specific to software documentation and are designed to make writing easier for anyone. Those new to user documentation will find the basics they need. Experienced documentation writers will refresh their memories and perhaps discover some new techniques.

CHAPTER 15

Building Paragraphs and Passages

Five simple guidelines will help you compose effective paragraphs, passages, and chapters:

- ○ Introduce each new topic.
- ○ Use transitions.
- ○ Arrange information in a logical order.
- ○ Include helpful headings.
- ○ Use lists for procedures and series of items.

INTRODUCING A NEW TOPIC

When you introduce a new topic, let your audience know what it is right away. You can use the following structure for a paragraph covering a simple topic:

1. Introduce the topic.

2. Discuss the topic.

3. Conclude or summarize the discussion when necessary.

Figure 15.1 illustrates the structure of a paragraph covering a simple topic.

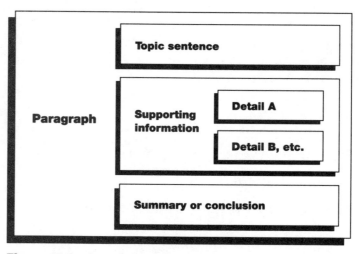

Figure 15.1. Structure of a Simple Paragraph.

Here, from *Reading and Me*, is an example of a paragraph with a topic sentence, discussion, and conclusion:

Many children have experimented with some of the reading readiness skills by the time they are three or four years old. While playing, they've sorted and identified things that are the "same," "different," and those that "do not belong." <u>Reading and Me</u> builds on these concrete experiences by challenging children to use these discrimination skills to classify familiar objects on the screen. These readiness skills will be essential as children learn to discriminate letters, sounds, and words.

More often, you'll introduce a topic with a topic paragraph and then explore two or more subtopics in the next few paragraphs. Sometimes you'll need to summarize your discussion before you move on to the next topic, but typically you'll let your headings mark the boundaries between topics.

In Figure 15.2, an excerpt from *Learning Aldus Free-Hand*, a topic paragraph introduces the subject—the illustration window—and then lists three subtopics: the illustration page, the pasteboard, and the toolbox.

MAKING TRANSITIONS

Transitions, which express relationships between one idea and another, help readers follow your train of thought. They tell readers that you're changing the topic, saying more about the topic, showing a contrast, and so on. We describe three types of transitions in this section: transitional words and phrases, repetition of key words and phrases, and parallelism.

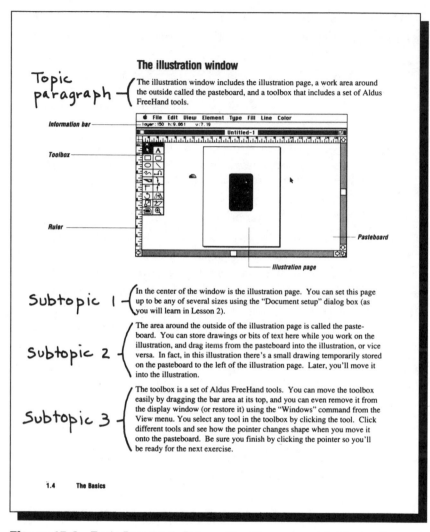

Figure 15.2. Topic Paragraph Followed by Discussion of Subtopics (from *Learning Aldus FreeHand*).

TRANSITIONAL WORDS AND PHRASES

Transitional words and phrases such as the following ease the flow of ideas:

if	for example	another way
because	for instance	once
unless	after	in addition
but	before	similarly
however	therefore	now
then	until	later
formerly	instead	otherwise

See how the transitional words and phrases (in bold type) in this excerpt from *Xerox Ventura Publisher Reference Guide* link the ideas in the paragraph:

NEWSLETTERS

These documents contain many text files, each representing a different article or story. The text in these documents does not usually flow consecutively from one column to the next, **but instead** skips columns or pages (e.g., the text on one page of a newspaper continues on the back page). Typography, **however**, is similar on every page in that the same fonts include newsletters, newspapers, magazines, and some types of brochures.

REPETITION OF KEY WORDS AND PHRASES

Repeat the key word or phrases every so often to keep readers focused on the topic. One simple way to do this is to conclude a paragraph by listing the points that the subsequent passages will cover.

Here, from *R:BASE for DOS User's Manual*, is an example that illustrates the use of both transitional phrases and repetition of key words. (The transitions are emphasized with bold type.)

> If you use **breakpoints** to display subtotals, you must define your subtotal fields as variables and reset them to zero after each breakpoint.
>
> **For example**, the sample report *slsrpt2* contains three **breakpoints**. The first **breakpoint**, defined as the column *empid*, groups data on the report by sales representatives' employee identification numbers. The **breakpoint also** generates subtotals for the price, freight, tax, and invoice total of each sales representative's transactions. The variables used to calculate the subtotals are *slsprice, slsfgt, slstax,* and *slsinv*. The variables must be reset to zero to ensure that subtotals do not accumulate throughout the report; that is, that subtotals for the first sales representative shown on the report are not added to subtotals for the second representative, and so on.
>
> The same is true for the report's second **breakpoint**, the *custid* column. . . .

PARALLELISM

Parallelism links ideas by repeating grammatical structure. You can use parallelism to link ideas within a sentence or a paragraph and also to link two or more separate paragraphs. The most common way to use parallelism is in a sentence containing a series. In the example that follows, each item in the series begins with an active verb:

> Once you establish the pattern, you can **copy** the design, **save** time and money, **improve** training procedures, and **instill** confidence in the operators.

Here, from *R:BASE for DOS User's Manual*, is an example of parallelism. The relevant phrases, each beginning with the words "When you," are emphasized with bold type.

(Strictly speaking, when you repeat whole sentence begin-nings, you're using a type of parallelism called *anaphora*.)

When you choose Expression from the Form Definition Menu, Forms EXPRESS displays this menu above a list of the defined expressions. . . .

   O *Define* displays all your expressions. You can enter new or change existing expressions.

   O *Customize lookups* is used to customize the characteristics of lookup expressions.

   O *Delete* is used to delete expressions.

   O *Retype* is used to change the data type of expressions associated with variables.

   O *Reorder* is used to reorder your list of expressions.

When you use your form with the ENTER command, you can display values that R:BASE looks up in the current table (master lookups), values looked up in other tables (standard lookups), or values that are the result of calculations.

When you use your form with the EDIT USING command, you can use fields. . . .

USING A LOGICAL ORDER

When arranging details in a passage, keep them in a logical order. For instance, if you're describing a screen display, the logical order to use is spatial; you start at the top, describe the first line, and then proceed downward. Other impor-tant logical orders are chronological order, order of impor-tance, and order of utility.

CHRONOLOGICAL ORDER

You use chronological order, of course, to write procedures. You also use it to describe a process or to tell readers what happened. In this example, from *Microsoft QuickC Programmer's Guide*, the writer uses chronological order to describe a process:

> The switch statement takes the place of a large number of nested if and else clauses. The switch statement transfers control to a statement within its body. The statement receiving control is the statement whose case constant expression (an integer or character constant, or a constant expression) matches the value of the switch test expression. Execution begins at the selected statement and continues through the end of the body or until a statement transfers control out of the switch body. Use the break statement to end processing of a particular case within the switch statement. Without the break, the program falls through to the next case.

ORDER OF UTILITY

Use the order of utility to give readers background necessary to understand or make use of information to follow, as in this example from *Microsoft QuickC Programmer's Guide*, where the writer explains EGA color graphics modes before telling the users how to remap colors:

> ○ **EGA color graphics modes**
>
> In a graphics mode, a pixel can be represented as a one-, two-, or four-bit value depending upon the mode selected. This representation is known as the "pixel value." In addition to the pixel value there is an ordinal color representation. Each color that can be displayed in a particular video mode is represented by a unique ordinal value. The mapping of pixel values onto the actual display colors produces a "palette" of colors that can be displayed.

A palette of colors is available whenever one of the EGA graphics modes is used. The EGA palettes may be remapped and redefined by the program. The default palette for the EGA modes is the same as the palette for the color text modes.

○ **Remapping individual colors**

Use the _remappalette function to remap one pixel value to a specified color, which must be a color supported by the current video mode. For example, the function below remaps the pixel value 1 to the value _RED. After this statement, whatever was displayed as blue will now appear as red:

```
_remappalette (1, _RED); /* reassign blue to red */
```

ORDER OF IMPORTANCE

Use the order of importance to give readers a sense of which details are important or to give details needed by the greatest number of readers. If you were listing modems, for instance, you would list the most commonly used ones first and the more exotic ones last.

In this example, from *Xerox Ventura Publisher Reference Guide*, the information on cables is arranged in order of descending importance. The writer begins with the equipment used by a majority of readers and proceeds to the less common equipment.

Whenever possible, connect your PostScript printer or typesetter using a Centronics-type parallel cable.

The IBM 4216 uses its own special cable.

If your PostScript printer or typesetter must be connected using an RS-232C cable, you should use the same cable for HP LaserJet. This cable can be purchased from Hewlett-Packard. The HP part number for the RS-232C serial cable is part number 92219J or 17255D. Connection of this serial cable to the IBM AT (9 pin) requires the IBM Serial Device Adapter Cable (IBM part number 6450217 or 6450242.) Some devices (such as the

Linotronic typesetters) may require a different sex connector at the printer end than provided with the HP cable. In this case, you must build your own cable.

If you want to build your own cables, Figures F-6 and F-7 show the correct wiring diagram for both PC (25 pin connectors) and AT (9 pin) machines.

WRITING HEADINGS

To write headings that serve as useful guideposts to your readers,

- Use headings whenever they are needed, to announce first-level topics, second-level topics, and, if necessary, third-level topics.

- Use at least two second-level headings under a first-level heading if you are going to classify or partition the topic at all. This guideline also applies to third-level headings.

- Make your headings specific and concrete; avoid vague generalities, whimsy, or cuteness.

- Keep your headings brief, if possible, because a brief heading is easier to read. Clarity comes first, however; never sacrifice it for brevity.

- If possible, make your headings consistent. For example, if one heading is a gerund like "Saving the File," make all the headings gerunds ("Backing Up the Disk," "Making Copies of the File," etc.). However, specific and helpful headings are more important than consistency; don't try to force headings into a pattern that doesn't help readers locate information.

Here, from *Amí User's Guide*, are examples of useful headings in a chapter called "How to Use Frames." Users can tell from the headings exactly what each section contains.

What Is a Frame?
How to Add a Frame
How to Select a Frame
How to Move, Re-Size, or Delete a Frame
   To Move a Frame on the Same Page
   To Move a Frame to Another Page
   To Move Multiple Frames
   To Re-Size a Frame
   To Delete a Frame
How to Move Overlapping Frames to the Front and Back
How Text Wraps Around a Frame
How to Modify a Frame's Layout
   Modifying a Frame's Borders
   Modifying a Frame's Lines
   Modifying a Frame's Columns and Tabs
How to Type in a Frame
How to Import Graphics into a Frame
   How to Scale Graphics in a Frame
   How to Move Graphics Within a Frame

USING LISTS FOR SERIES AND PROCEDURES

Procedures are easier for readers to follow when you arrange them in numbered or lettered lists. A series of related facts or details is also easier to read when you itemize the details in a list using bullets or numbers.

Here are guidelines for writing a list:

○ Start your list with an introductory sentence.

○ Use parallel grammatical structure.

○ Be consistent with punctuation and capitalization.

○ Limit the number of items in a list to eight.

○ Number the steps in instructions or procedures.

○ Number or letter list items when they need to be in chronological order or prioritized or when you need to refer to them in other parts of the document. Otherwise, use bullets or dashes.

This example, from *Xerox Ventura Publisher Reference Guide*, lists a series of items:

Frames can be anchored in one of four ways:
    ○ Fixed, on the same page
    ○ Relative, above the anchor location
    ○ Relative, below the anchor location
    ○ Relative, automatically at anchor

The same information would be harder to absorb, or ever find again, if it were written in a solid paragraph:

Frames can be anchored in one of four ways: fixed, on the same page; relative, above the anchor location; relative, below the anchor location; and relative, automatically at anchor.

Here, again from *Xerox Ventura Publisher Reference Guide*, is an example of a procedure:

> You must do the following to place text or picture files on the page or in a specific frame:
>
>   1. Select the Frame mode.
>   2. Select the frame or page where you want the text or graphic to appear.
>   3. Select the file name from the list of files in the Assignment list.

To show you how much more effective the procedure is when it is in the form of a numbered list, we have rewritten it as a solid paragraph.

> To place text or picture files on the page or in a specific frame, you must select the Frame mode, select the frame or page where you want the text or graphic to appear, and select the frame name from the list of files in the Assignment list.

Follow the techniques described in this chapter to build solid paragraphs and passages, and you will have a solid document. (See Chapter 19, "Writing Procedures," for information on how to write procedures and Chapter 5, "Setting Standards," for information on setting the style for lists and procedures.)

CHAPTER 16

Writing from the Readers' Viewpoint

Have you ever read a manual that seemed stilted or condescending? Or one that was written with technical jargon that only a handful of people in the whole world could possibly understand? Because the language in the manual didn't reflect your attitude or your level of knowledge about the subject, you were probably either bored or annoyed. To avoid boring or annoying *your* readers, use the following guidelines to tailor language to your readers:

- ○ Use semiformal English.
- ○ Project a helpful but respectful attitude.
- ○ Maintain the appropriate level of technicality.
- ○ Explain the relevance of the information.
- ○ Use nonsexist language.

USING SEMIFORMAL ENGLISH

We commonly use three varieties of English in all types of written communications: informal, formal, and semiformal. For software documentation, informal English is too casual and formal English is too stuffy. Semiformal English is the appropriate choice.

To make language in your software documentation semiformal,

○ Speak directly to the readers in a conversational tone. Use the personal pronoun *you*.

○ Use short, plain words rather than long, fancy ones—*pay* rather than *recompense*, for instance.

○ Use specific and concrete terms rather than general terms and abstractions—*memos* rather than *communications*, for instance.

○ Use phrases from everyday speech, like "look into" and "spell out." Use *and, so,* and *that* instead of *furthermore, consequently,* and *wherein*.

○ Use contractions occasionally, such as *it's* or *you're*.

The following excerpt from the *Ami User's Guide* is a good example. Notice the conversational tone, the use of the word *you*, the contractions, and the simple, straightforward language.

File/Exit

Exits Ami.

If you haven't saved changes made to the document, you're given the chance to do so. If you've been working in an "untitled" document, the SAVE AS ... dialog box appears so that you can name the document. If you don't want to save the document, click on No.

Here's another example, this one from *Microsoft QuickBASIC: Programming in BASIC*. Although the subject matter is technical, the writer addresses the readers directly and uses a conversational tone.

While BASICA's single-line **IF . . . THEN . . . ELSE** is adequate for simple decisions, it can lead to virtually unreadable code in cases of more complicated ones. This is especially true if you write your programs so all alternative actions take place with the **IF . . . THEN . . . ELSE** statement itself or if you nest **IF . . . THEN . . . ELSE** statements (that is, if you put one **IF . . . THEN . . . ELSE** inside another, a perfectly legal construction).

SHOWING RESPECT FOR THE READERS

Address readers as if they are your peers in intelligence and ability to comprehend the material. You are the person who has the specific knowledge that they need and you're happy to explain the program or the system to them. Avoid the simplistic or patronizing tone that results when you use a long string of very simple sentences, repeat instructions too often, or elaborate over the obvious.

In the following example, from *Aldus SnapShot User Manual*, the writer deftly handles the delicate matter of warning the readers about a potential mistake, without any exhortations or lectures:

After you freeze the image, you can save it immediately, or you can modify the image first, and then save it. But remember that the frozen image isn't saved until you've used the "Save image . . ." command from the File menu. If you have not yet frozen the image, "Save image . . ." is grayed.

USING THE APPROPRIATE LEVEL OF TECHNICALITY

The technical level of your language depends on the readers' knowledge of your subject. You can follow these guidelines:

○ Define any terms that may be new to readers.

○ Provide background material that will help readers understand the information—but only to the degree that's necessary. If they don't need details, leave them out.

○ Leave out theory, no matter how fascinating, if it doesn't help accomplish the document's goals.

○ Keep background material and explanations at the level your readers need.

○ Give readers only the technical details necessary to accomplish the goals of the document.

○ If your readers have varying levels of knowledge, write for those who are the least knowledgeable.

Here are three examples from *R:BASE for DOS* documentation: one from a manual for novices, one from a guide for more experienced users, and one from a reference manual of technical information. Each excerpt introduces the same subject—expressions—but at differing levels of technicality.

In the first example, from *R:BASE Learning Guide*, the writer begins by giving novice users necessary background information on both variables and expressions, defining both terms, and then gives the users a sampling of what expressions are used for.

TECHNICAL LEVEL FOR NOVICE USERS:

USING VARIABLES AND EXPRESSIONS

Variables have many uses in the R:BASE command mode and EXPRESS modules. You can define variables or use expressions to calculate subtotals and totals, manipulate text values, draw data from tables, perform complex mathematical operations, return financial data such as interest rates, or perform many other functions.

A variable is an item that holds data. It is similar to a column, except that a variable is not connected to any particular table in a database. You can define a variable at the R> prompt and then use the contents of the variable with more than one database. Variables, then, are global with R:BASE.

An expression is the computation that gives a variable its value. Expressions can also provide the value of a column as in computed columns (discussed in lesson 2), or they can be used to calculate values on the fly with the SELECT command.

In the next example, from the *R:BASE User's Manual,* the writer quickly gets into specific detail about using expressions. Although the writer defines the term *expressions,* he or she assumes that users are familiar with other terms, such as *syntax, value, operators* and *operands,* and *arguments.* The writer also includes an example to help readers apply what they've just learned.

TECHNICAL LEVEL FOR INTERMEDIATE USERS:

USING EXPRESSIONS

Several R:BASE commands use expressions as part of their syntax for the following purposes:

- ○ In WHERE clauses to specify rows to process
- ○ To SET the value of a variable
- ○ As the definition of a computer column (see chapter 2, "Database Definition," in this manual)
- ○ To define a temporary display column (see chapter 5, "Data Output Using R:BASE Commands," in this manual)

○ To calculate or recalculate the value of a column (see chapter 3, "Data Entry and Modification," in this manual)

○ In IF and WHILE structures as a condition of processing (see chapter 3, "Programming in R:BASE," in <u>Building Applications</u>)

Expressions are calculations used to determine a value. An expression can contain multiple operators and operands. If an expression contains spaces as arguments, include them within double quotation marks (" "). If a text argument in an expression contains spaces, include it within double quotation marks so that it is treated as a single item. Constants used in expressions must be enclosed in double quotation marks if they contain any of the following separators: (,), **, *, +, &, %, /, -, or comma. For example, if you include a date constant in an expression, you must enclose the date in quotation marks like this:

SET VAR vduedate TO ("6/16/87" + 30)

If the quotation marks are not included, R:BASE could interpret the above expression to mean divide 6 by 16 then divide by 87 and, finally, add 30.

In the third example, which shows appropriate technicality in language for advanced users, the writer defines the term *expressions* but assumes that users understand the other terms. The writer gives a lot of detail that, presumably, users at this level need but that would only muddy the waters for less knowledgeable users. For instance, users learn the specific limits on the use of expressions. Although assuming that users know what expressions are used for, the writer includes a reference to another document just in case. The excerpt is from *R:BASE Building Applications/ Command Dictionary*:

TECHNICAL LEVEL FOR ADVANCED USERS:

EXPRESSIONS

Expressions are calculations used to determine a value. An expression may contain multiple operators, operands, and functions. Spaces are not required. However, if an expression contains spaces or is a text string, it must be enclosed in parentheses or double quotation marks. For clarity, the examples in this manual are shown with internal spaces between operands and operators, and each expression is surrounded with parentheses.

Expressions can be up to 160 characters long and can contain a combination of up to 50 operators, operands, and functions. Each command that can use an expression can have up to 20. For a complete discussion of expressions, see chapter 1, "R:BASE Fundamentals," in the User's Manual.

Be sure that constants that contain any separator characters (+, -, *, /, **, &, (,), or comma) are contained within quotation marks. This includes text strings and dates. For example, use the following format to include a date in an expression:

SET VAR duedate = ("06/15/87" + 30)

Otherwise, R:BASE will interpret the slashes (/) in the date as division operators.

EXPLAINING RELEVANCE

Readers absorb information more readily when they understand why it's relevant for them. Before you jump into detailed explanations or instructions, tell readers why they need the information, or give them a "for instance" example explaining how they might use it.

Here, from *Rapid Relay User Manual*, is a good example:

EXPLAINING RELEVANCE:

PICKING FROM A DIRECTORY "TREE"

If you work with a hard disk, you may not remember the exact name of the directory you want to use, especially if you have many directory names. Rapid Relay can help you. Instead of typing the directory name you want, you can tell Rapid Relay to show you a menu of all the directories on the current disk, and you can pick the one you want.

After picking the Directory command from the main menu, press the F2 key. Rapid Relay will display a "tree" showing the names of all the directories (Figure 6).

To see how flat and uninvolving information can be when you don't explain its relevance, let's rewrite this passage, leaving out the explanatory preface.

FAILING TO EXPLAIN RELEVANCE:

PICKING FROM A DIRECTORY "TREE"

To see a menu of all the directories on the current disk, pick the Directory command from the main menu and press the F2 key. Rapid Relay will display a "tree" showing the names of all the directories.

In this next excerpt from *PFS: First Choice® Version 3.02*, the writer involves the readers by first mentioning circumstances in which they might need the Change form design procedure.

After you have used your database for some time, you may wish you had included another field, or you may want to change the position of a field on the form design. With First Choice, you can redesign the form to suit your changing needs. You can add, erase, or change field names and move the fields around. You can also change the background text and field types.

Before you redesign your form, you should know the following:

- ○ Always make a spare copy of your database. Occasionally, information may be lost during the redesign process.

- ○ It may take a long time for First Choice to redesign your records, depending on the complexity of the design, the amount of information in the records, and the number of records.

- ○ If you erase a field, the information you put in that field will be lost from every record in the database.

- ○ Any changes you make to the form design may affect a form program, report, or table view instructions you've saved for the database.

USING NONSEXIST LANGUAGE

Most organizations have adopted guidelines for keeping sexism out of the language in their communications. If your organization hasn't established such guidelines, you can use the ones below.

GENERIC TITLES AND DESCRIPTIONS

Choose titles and descriptive words that are not gender-specific, as in the following examples:

USE	RATHER THAN
supervisor, chief	foreman
service representative, technician	repairman
businessperson	businessman
chair, chairperson	chairman
representative	spokesman
worker	workman
assistant, key aide	right-hand man
flight attendant	stewardess
drafter	draftsman
big job	man-sized job
humans, humankind, people	mankind

NONSEXIST PRONOUNS AND ADJECTIVES

Use pronouns that aren't exclusively male or female. Here are some simple techniques to help you address 100 percent of your readers.

Address the readers directly, if possible (*You can repeat the procedure* instead of *He can repeat the procedure*). Here's an example from the *who·what·when User's Manual*.

> When you make entries into the Daily Calendar, they are for the person and the date displayed at the top of the screen. Although most people only track their own Daily Calendar and that of one or two other people, it is possible to display a Daily Calendar for anyone you have entered into **who·what·when**.

Use the plural form rather than the singular (*programmers keep their workbooks* instead of *a programmer keeps his workbook*). Here's an example from *Microsoft QuickBASIC:*

> QuickBASIC is a powerful development tool for professional use. Yet it is also the ideal language for beginning and intermediate programmers—people who aren't professional programmers but need a language that helps them reach their programming goals efficiently.

If the title has to be singular, substitute an article (a, an, the) for a pronoun (*the operator enters a password* instead of *the operator enters his password*). Here's an example:

> Enter the number of federal allowances claimed by the employee on the federal W-4 form.

Repeat the title of the person rather than using a pronoun (*The accountant knows the procedure. When the accountant updates . . .* instead of *The accountant knows the procedure. When he . . .*). Here's an example from *Xerox Ventura Publisher Workbook:*

> It is really up to the speaker to deliver an effective presentation, but without professional support material, a good speaker must struggle to keep the audience's eyes and ears pointed toward the podium.

If you can find no other way to avoid a sexist term, use *he/she* or *him/her*. Here's an example from the *who·what· when User's Manual*.

Wanting to be well prepared, you print out a People View Calendar, which cross-references all the tasks that you are doing with your boss and you review your commitments with him or her.

You'll find that avoiding sexist usages, along with choosing appropriate language, gives readers confidence in your ability to teach them how to use the software.

CHAPTER 17

Using Clear and Strong Language

If you want users to get the most out of the software program, use language that is clear, strong, and direct. When you practice the four simple techniques described in this chapter, users will be able to grasp your explanations, follow your procedures, and use the software to its full capabilities. To write with strength and clarity,

- O use plain language
- O eliminate unnecessary words
- O use active verbs
- O write in the proper tense

USING PLAIN ENGLISH

To provide the highest level of clarity to your readers, use plain English. You can follow these two simple guidelines:

- ○ Use short sentences predominantly, mixing in a few longer ones to avoid monotony.

- ○ Use plain one- and two-syllable words rather than three- and four-syllable words whenever possible.

WRITING SHORT SENTENCES

The following paragraph is hard to read because of two overly long, run-on sentences.

LONG, COMPLICATED SENTENCES:

This program prints a column of figures, but you can see that some of the figures have decimal points while others don't and that the decimal points don't line up properly. For your next exercise, write a program that will add a decimal point and two zeros to each of the even dollar figures, align all of the decimal points, and either get rid of any blank space that falls between a "$" and a number or align all of the dollar signs in one column.

In the rewrite, the information is easier to follow when the two sentences become five.

SHORTER, EASIER-TO-FOLLOW SENTENCES:

This program prints a column of figures, but you can see that some of the figures have decimal points and others don't. In addition, the decimal points don't line up properly. For your next exercise, write a program to bring order to this column of figures. Add a decimal point and two zeros to each of the even dollar figures, and align all of the decimal points. Either get rid of any blank space that falls between a "$" and a number, or align all of the dollar signs in one column.

CHOOSING PLAIN WORDS

Use common words, preferably with one or two syllables, rather than fancy words. Here are some examples to show you what we mean:

USE	INSTEAD OF
say, write, tell	communicate
do	implement
show, point out	indicate
help, assist	facilitate
try	attempt
find out, discover, set, learn	ascertain
buy	procure
permit, call for	warrant
by, following, per, under	pursuant to
rank	prioritize
method	methodology
best, most, greatest	optimum
meet, work with	interface with
end	expiration
speed up, hasten	expedite
fair	equitable
give, issue, pass	disseminate
near	close proximity
is, makes up	constitutes

ELIMINATING UNNECESSARY WORDS

You can make your language more readable by eliminating unnecessary words, such as

- O noun clusters (use *classroom* instead of *structured learning environment*)
- O prepositional phrases (use *because* instead of *as a result of*)
- O redundancies (use *repeat* instead of *repeat again*)
- O wordy phrases (use *truth* instead of *plain, unvarnished truth*)

Below we list some examples of noun clusters, prepositional phrases, redundancies, and wordy phrases, along with some simpler words to replace them:

ELIMINATE NOUN CLUSTERS:

USE	INSTEAD OF
problems	design constraints considerations
mistake	quality reduction factor

ELIMINATE PREPOSITIONAL PHRASES:

USE	INSTEAD OF
about	of the order of magnitude of
more than	in excess of
because	as a result of
know	be aware of the fact that

now	at this point in time
to	in order to
for	for the purpose of
about, regarding	in reference to

ELIMINATE REDUNDANCIES:

USE	*INSTEAD OF*
available	currently available
current, existing	currently existing
eliminate, end	eliminate completely
spell out, explain	spell out in detail
small	small in size
yellow	yellow in color
essential, necessary	absolutely essential
different	various different
conclusion, end	final conclusion
introduce	first introduce
without	totally devoid of
entering	first entering
straight, linear	straight linear
consensus	general consensus
innovation	new innovation
near	close proximity
oval	oval in shape

right, proper	right and proper
halves	two equal halves
reason	reason why
cooperation	mutual cooperation
result	end result
continue	continue on

ELIMINATE WORDY PHRASES:

USE	*INSTEAD OF*
because	due to the fact that
most	the majority of
could	would be able to
obvious	readily apparent
indicate, show	be an indication of
must	it is essential that
remind you	call your attention to the fact that
allow	afford an opportunity

These lists contain only a few examples to remind you to look for noun clusters, prepositional phrases, redundancies, and just plain wordiness. You'll run into many more examples—we are all guilty of wordiness—so be alert and watch out for them in your writing.

We'd like to show what can happen when you don't use simple language. Here, from *PFS: First Choice® Version 3.02*, is a paragraph written in plain English. We then rewrote the same paragraph, substituting fancy words and phrases.

PLAIN LANGUAGE:

First Choice can produce special reports: reports showing only the results of calculations and reports combining the results of one or more columns, to produce derived columns.

REWRITTEN WITH FANCY LANGUAGE:

First Choice facilitates the production of different and distinctive reports: reports exhibiting the end results of calculations exclusively and reports combining together the results of one or more columns to generate derived columns.

USING ACTIVE VERBS

Use active verbs in most of your sentences to make your style forceful and direct. Using passive verbs weakens your language and makes it seem vague and lacking in authority.

ACTIVE:

The operator must <u>sign</u> the sheet.

PASSIVE:

The sheet must <u>be signed</u> by the operator.

ACTIVE:

The lead operator <u>changes</u> the password.

PASSIVE:

The password <u>is changed</u> by the lead operator.

When you read your drafts, look for words like *is, was, are, be, is being, are being,* and *have been* in your sentences.

See if you can replace them with active verbs to make the sentence more direct and energetic.

Here is a paragraph from *Rapid Relay User's Guide*, first in its original form and then rewritten to demonstrate how the use of passive verbs weakens it.

ACTIVE VERBS:

Rapid Relay provides convenient commands for performing almost all routine DOS file and directory functions. You can also execute any DOS command from Rapid Relay, without exiting to DOS. In fact, you can give as many DOS commands as you wish and then take up where you left off in Rapid Relay.

REWRITTEN WITH PASSIVE VERBS:

Convenient commands are provided by Rapid Relay for performing almost all routine DOS file and directory functions. Any DOS command can also be executed from Rapid Relay, without exiting to DOS. In fact, as many DOS commands as you wish can be given and Rapid Relay taken up where you left off.

In a few cases, however, you'll want to use a passive verb: when the agent is unknown or when you need to be indirect and impersonal to avoid offending someone.

ACCEPTABLE PASSIVE VERB:

Unauthorized versions were widely distributed.

CHOOSING THE PROPER TENSE

Use the present tense most of the time; it's always appropriate when you're giving instructions, presenting general information, or explaining principles and theories.

It's very easy to slip into the future tense when you're thinking about users and how they *will* use the program, but guard against the tendency because it weakens your writing. Use the future tense only when you write about what's going to or what could happen. In the following example, you can see that the first version sounds more confident and authoritative than the second.

PRESENT TENSE:

To write a program, first type the command NEW. This command erases any program already in memory.

IMPROPER USE OF THE FUTURE TENSE:

If you're going to write a program, your first step will be to type the command NEW. This command will erase any program already in memory.

Here's an example of the proper use of the future tense:

PROPER USE OF THE FUTURE TENSE:

When you initiate the program using the procedure described above, you won't have any problems.

When you use plain English, delete unnecessary words, and use active verbs and the proper tense, you give strength and clarity to all your documents.

CHAPTER 18

Explaining, Describing, and Defining

When you introduce a new concept, function, or procedure to your readers, you usually begin with an explanation that includes definitions and descriptions. This chapter contains guidelines to help you define, describe, and explain clearly and effectively.

EXPLAINING AND DESCRIBING

When you explain and describe new concepts or functions, use these guidelines:

○ Introduce the explanation or description with a limiting title (a heading may serve as the title). For instance, use *Typing Measurements in Dialog Boxes* rather than *Measuring Text*.

○ Give readers an overview before getting into the details. After the overview, list the subtopics and then describe each subtopic.

○ Define any terms new to the users. (We give guidelines for defining terms later in the chapter.)

○ Use illustrations and examples if they'll make the description or the explanation clearer.

○ Use an appropriate logical order to arrange the details: spatial order for objects like screens or printers, chronological order for processes or events.

Figures 18.1 through 18.5 show how writers develop effective explanations and descriptions, using examples and illustrations.

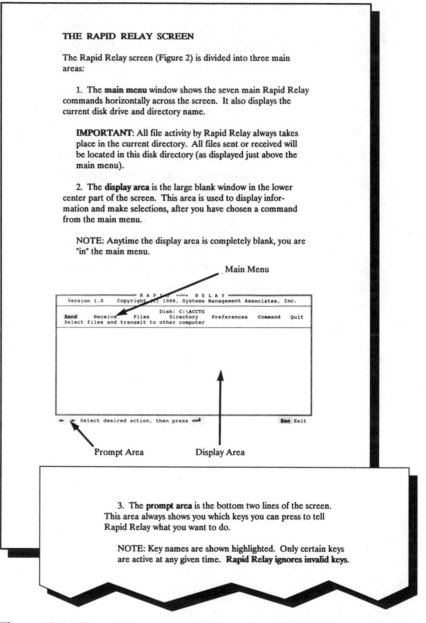

THE RAPID RELAY SCREEN

The Rapid Relay screen (Figure 2) is divided into three main areas:

1. The **main menu** window shows the seven main Rapid Relay commands horizontally across the screen. It also displays the current disk drive and directory name.

IMPORTANT: All file activity by Rapid Relay always takes place in the current directory. All files sent or received will be located in this disk directory (as displayed just above the main menu).

2. The **display area** is the large blank window in the lower center part of the screen. This area is used to display information and make selections, after you have chosen a command from the main menu.

NOTE: Anytime the display area is completely blank, you are "in" the main menu.

Main Menu

```
═════════════ R A P I D ←═══→ R E L A Y ═════════════
Version 1.0    Copyright (c) 1988, Systems Management Associates, Inc.
                            Disk: C:\ACCTS
Send     Receive     Files       Directory     Preferences   Command    Quit
Select files and transmit to other computer



→  ← Select desired action, then press ←┘                      Esc Exit
```

Prompt Area   Display Area

3. The **prompt area** is the bottom two lines of the screen. This area always shows you which keys you can press to tell Rapid Relay what you want to do.

NOTE: Key names are shown highlighted. Only certain keys are active at any given time. **Rapid Relay ignores invalid keys.**

Figure 18.1. Descriptions and Explanations (from *Rapid Relay User Manual*). The writer describes the screen using a limiting title, spatial order, several definitions (the defined terms are in bold type), and an illustration.

9.2.1.2 File-Name Extensions

A DOS file name has two parts: the "base name," which includes everything before the period (.); and the "extension," which includes the period and up to three characters following the period. The extension identifies the type of the file.

The **QCL** command uses the extension of each file name to determine how to process the corresponding file, as explained in the following list:

Extension	Processing
.C	**QCL** assumes the file is a C source file and compiles it
.OBJ	**QCL** assumes the file is an object file and passes it to the linker for linking
.LIB	**QCL** assumes the file is a stand-alone library and passes it to the linker for linking with the generated object files and the object files given on the command line
Any other extension or no extension	**QCL** assumes the file is an object file and passes it to the linker for linking

■ **Example**

The command line

```
QCL A.C B.C C.OBJ D
```

compiles the files A.C and B.C, creating object files named A.OBJ and B.OBJ. These object files are then linked with C.OBJ and D.OBJ to form an executable file named A.EXE (since the base name of the first file on the command line is A). Note that the extension .OBJ is assumed for D since no extension is given on the command line.

Figure 18.2. Descriptions and Explanations (from *Microsoft QuickC Programmer's Guide*). An example helps explain filename extensions.

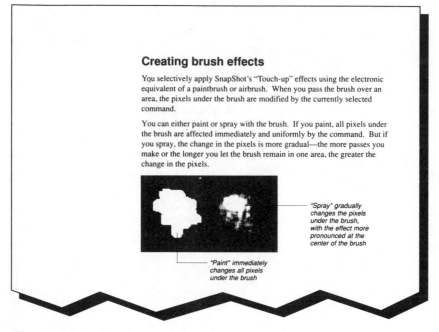

Creating brush effects

You selectively apply SnapShot's "Touch-up" effects using the electronic equivalent of a paintbrush or airbrush. When you pass the brush over an area, the pixels under the brush are modified by the currently selected command.

You can either paint or spray with the brush. If you paint, all pixels under the brush are affected immediately and uniformly by the command. But if you spray, the change in the pixels is more gradual—the more passes you make or the longer you let the brush remain in one area, the greater the change in the pixels.

"Spray" gradually changes the pixels under the brush, with the effect more pronounced at the center of the brush

"Paint" immediately changes all pixels under the brush

Figure 18.3. Descriptions and Explanations (from *Aldus SnapShot User Manual*). Words alone can't explain the difference between *paint* and *spray*, but an illustration can.

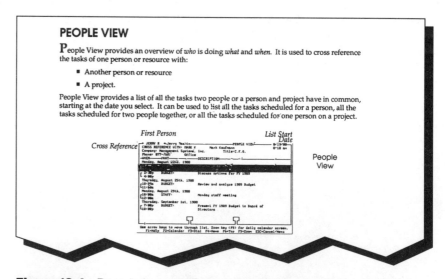

PEOPLE VIEW

People View provides an overview of *who* is doing *what* and *when*. It is used to cross reference the tasks of one person or resource with:

- Another person or resource
- A project.

People View provides a list of all the tasks two people or a person and project have in common, starting at the date you select. It can be used to list all the tasks scheduled for a person, all the tasks scheduled for two people together, or all the tasks scheduled for one person on a project.

Figure 18.4. Descriptions and Explanations (from *who·what·when User's Manual*). The writer explains "People View." Note the limiting title, the overview, and the use of an illustration as an example.

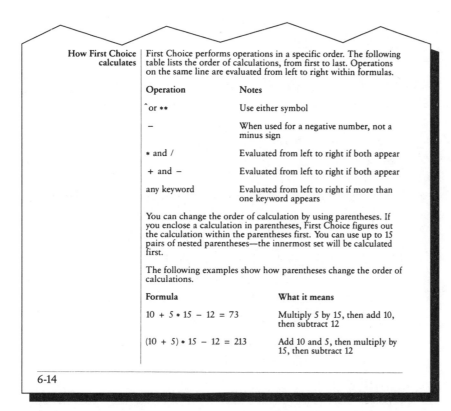

How First Choice calculates

First Choice performs operations in a specific order. The following table lists the order of calculations, from first to last. Operations on the same line are evaluated from left to right within formulas.

Operation	Notes
ˆ or **	Use either symbol
−	When used for a negative number, not a minus sign
* and /	Evaluated from left to right if both appear
+ and −	Evaluated from left to right if both appear
any keyword	Evaluated from left to right if more than one keyword appears

You can change the order of calculation by using parentheses. If you enclose a calculation in parentheses, First Choice figures out the calculation within the parentheses first. You can use up to 15 pairs of nested parentheses—the innermost set will be calculated first.

The following examples show how parentheses change the order of calculations.

Formula	What it means
$10 + 5 * 15 − 12 = 73$	Multiply 5 by 15, then add 10, then subtract 12
$(10 + 5) * 15 − 12 = 213$	Add 10 and 5, then multiply by 15, then subtract 12

6-14

Figure 18.5. Descriptions and Explanations (from *PFS: First Choice®* Version 3.02). The writer describes how First Choice calculates. Note the limiting title, the overview, and the use of examples.

DEFINING TERMS

Your explanations and descriptions will often include definitions. Even if you provide a glossary or a page of definitions in your front matter, you need to define new terms in the text. The guidelines for effective definitions are as follows:

○ Define each new term immediately, the first time you mention it. When your manual is long, define the new term on first mention in each new section.

○ Add visual emphasis to the term, its definition, or both by italicizing, underlining, or putting quotation marks around the term or parentheses around the definition.

○ Provide examples, illustrations, or both if the concept is difficult to pin down.

Here, from *PFS: First Choice® Version 3.02,* are two examples of definitions. Each term is italicized, signaling that a definition is to follow.

DEFINITIONS:

With computers, anything you can type from the keyboard is called a *character.* A character can be a letter, number, space, punctuation mark, or symbol.

When you design a form, you are setting up a framework to store your information. Each item you include on this form is called a *field name.* (The field name plus the actual information that you fill in is called a *field.*)

Figures 18.6 and 18.7 are two final illustrations, showing how you can support your definitions with examples and illustrations.

Interactive on-screen kerning and tracking

Kerning is the process of moving letters closer together, and is usually used in headlines where certain letter combinations, such as a capital **V** followed by a capital **A**, appear to be too far apart when spaced with normal proportional spacing. For example, the **A** in the word **VALUE** is kerned in the second line on the next page.

Un-kerned text: **VALUE**

Kerned text: **VALUE**

Tracking is the process of moving *every* letter in a word or sentence either further apart or closer together.

Interactive kerning/tracking can be used in several ways to:

* Make text fit a give space.

* Improve the appearance of large headlines.

* Locally adjust typography without creating a new paragraph tag.

This feature is particularly useful in creating headlines and titles, since you can instantaneously see the effect of your changes on the overall

4-22   REFERENCE GUIDE

Figure 18.6. Definition with an Example (from *Xerox Ventura Publisher Reference Guide*). The writer defines the term *kerning*, setting the term off with bold type, and then uses an example to support the definition.

individu... ...sheet. However, ... it
refer to more th... ...cell at a time. With First Cho... ...u can
create *ranges* to refer to an area in a spreadsheet.

A range is several cells located next to each other within a
spreadsheet. A range can be a row, a column, or a group of rows or
columns, and you refer to the range by its coordinates, not by cell
names. You write the first and last coordinates for the range, and
separate them with two dots (..). For example, R10C10..R10C20 is

6-16

A range can be a row, a column, or a block of cells.

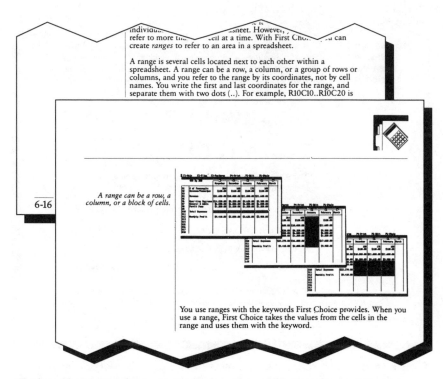

You use ranges with the keywords First Choice provides. When you
use a range, First Choice takes the values from the cells in the
range and uses them with the keyword.

Figure 18.7. Definition with Illustration (from *PFS: First Choice® Version
3.02*). The writer defines *range* (set off with italics) and shows the users several examples in the illustrations.

CHAPTER 19

Writing Procedures

Procedures are the heart of tutorials and procedures guides. Follow these guidelines to make sure your procedures are comprehensive and easy to follow:

- ○ Begin the procedure with a clear and limiting title.
- ○ Write complete instructions; include every step, and tell readers what will happen as well as what to do.
- ○ Organize procedures into lists of numbered steps.
- ○ Use parallel grammatical structure.
- ○ Limit the number of steps in your procedures to eight.
- ○ Use illustrations and examples to make the procedure clearer.

WRITING COMPLETE PROCEDURES

If it's going to be of the most help to readers, a procedure needs to be as complete as possible. Follow these guidelines:

○ Perform the task or watch someone else do it. Note every step, every result.

○ Assume nothing. Write down every step in the procedure.

○ Describe what happens as well as the actions to take. Describe the results of each action—what appears on the screen, for instance—*after* the reader carries out a command. If anything happens that might confuse readers, describe it so they won't be frustrated by uncertainty.

○ Test your procedures after you've written them. Conduct a usability test (described in Chapter 6, "Reviews, Usability Tests, and Revisions"), or try to find someone who matches the audience profile to test your procedures for you. Your next best option is to ask a co-worker to test your procedures. The least desirable option is to test them yourself.

USING NUMBERED STEPS

A procedure is easier to read when it's arranged in a numbered list rather than buried in solid paragraphs.

HARD-TO-READ PROCEDURE:

To select a format for your page numbers, first choose the PAGE LAYOUT command from the Format menu. Choose

Automatic Page Numbers and then select one of the options in Page Number Format. To carry out the command, press the Enter key.

EASY-TO-READ PROCEDURE:

To select a format for your page numbers:

1. Choose the **PAGE LAYOUT** command from the Format menu.
2. Choose Automatic Page Numbers.
3. Select one of the options in Page Number Format.
4. Press the Enter key to carry out the command.

USING PARALLEL GRAMMATICAL STRUCTURE

Use parallel grammatical structure in each step of the procedure so readers won't be confused. Generally a direct command, beginning with an action verb, eliminates any possible confusion about what to do. In the following example, steps 1, 3, and 5 are direct commands that begin with action verbs, while steps 2, 4, and 6 are not.

CONFUSING GRAMMATICAL STRUCTURE:

To add a new row:

1. Move the highlight into the row immediately below where you want the new row to appear.
2. Add Row/Column from the Edit menu is the next command chosen, and the Add Row/Column box appears.
3. Add a row by typing R.
4. You must now press the Tab key.
5. Type the number of rows you want to insert.
6. Pressing the Enter key will insert the rows.

In the rewrite of the procedure, each step—beginning with the action verbs *move, choose, type,* and *press*—is now a direct command:

PARALLEL GRAMMATICAL STRUCTURE:

To add a new row:

1. Move the highlight into the row immediately below where you want the new row to appear.
2. Choose Add Row/Column from the Edit menu. The Add Row/Column box appears.
3. Type R to add a row.
4. Press the Tab key.
5. Type the number of rows you want to insert.
6. Press the Enter key to add the rows.

LIMITING THE NUMBER OF STEPS

If possible, you should have no more than eight to ten steps in any procedure. If a procedure has more than ten steps, divide it into two or more procedures. For instance, 24 steps describing how to change the paper in a printer could be broken into three sets of instructions, one explaining how to remove the paper cartridge, one explaining how to load the new paper, and one explaining how to check that the paper has been loaded properly.

USING ILLUSTRATIONS AND EXAMPLES

An illustration or an example can make a procedure clear in a way that words alone cannot. For instance, when you tell users to set a switch to a specific location, an illustration that shows the exact location saves the reader time and uncertainty. And the illustration that comes after *Your screen should now look like this:* is invaluable in making procedures clear to readers.

When using an illustration to support a procedure, follow these two guidelines:

○ Keep the illustration simple and uncluttered.

○ Position the illustration as close as possible to the step or procedure it supports. If this isn't possible, tell readers where they can find the illustration. For example, you could write *See Figure 9.3 on the following page*.

Figure 19.1 shows a simple procedure that is supported by an illustration.

Sometimes, especially in language manuals, the procedures may be complex or hard to clarify with just words. In these instances, an example can help clear up any possible confusion. To write effective examples, follow these guidelines:

○ Choose examples appropriate to your readers' needs and level of knowledge.

○ Keep examples brief.

○ Choose examples that are as interesting and as relevant to your readers as possible.

Figure 19.2 shows just how an example can clarify a procedure.

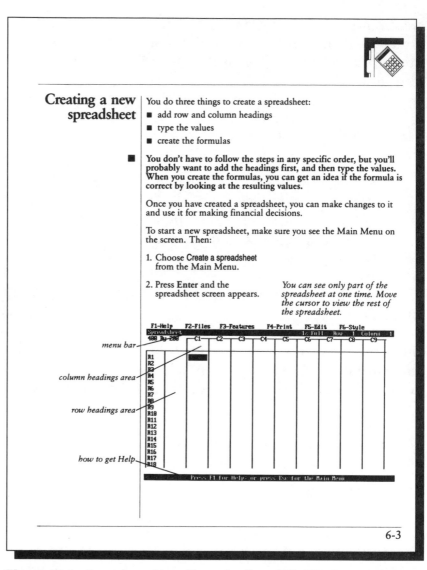

Creating a new spreadsheet

You do three things to create a spreadsheet:
- add row and column headings
- type the values
- create the formulas

You don't have to follow the steps in any specific order, but you'll probably want to add the headings first, and then type the values. When you create the formulas, you can get an idea if the formula is correct by looking at the resulting values.

Once you have created a spreadsheet, you can make changes to it and use it for making financial decisions.

To start a new spreadsheet, make sure you see the Main Menu on the screen. Then:

1. Choose **Create a spreadsheet** from the Main Menu.

2. Press **Enter** and the spreadsheet screen appears.

You can see only part of the spreadsheet at one time. Move the cursor to view the rest of the spreadsheet.

menu bar

column headings area

row headings area

how to get Help

6-3

Figure 19.1. Procedure with an Illustration (from *PFS: First Choice® Version 3.02*). Notice the specific title, "Creating a new spreadsheet," the action verbs that begin each step, and the clear and simple illustration.

Typing formulas with quick entry

Quick entry works with formulas, so that you can repeat a formula for several cells. If the formula refers to cells by their coordinates, First Choice changes the cell coordinates depending on the row or column you move to.

1. Move to the cell where you want to start typing a formula.

2. Choose Type or edit cell formula from the Features menu (or press **Alt-F**).

   The Formula box for the current cell appears.

3. Type the formula below Formula.

   You could use an existing formula as the starting formula.

4. Press **Alt-Q** to start quick entry.

5. Move to the next cell in the series.

   Use Enter, Ctrl-Enter, Tab, or Shift-Tab.

Quick entry stops when you press **Alt-Q** again. Pressing **Esc** cancels the formula in the current cell if you entered one.

For example, this formula in column 1 gets copied to column 2 as follows:

	C1		C2
Name:	Formula R1C1:	Name:	Formula R1C2:
	R2C1 + R7C1		R2C2 + R7C2

When you use quick entry with formulas, the cell coordinates increase as you move to the right or down; they decrease as you move to the left or up.

6-15

Figure 19.2. Procedure with an Example (from *PFS: First Choice® Version 3.02*). The procedure has a clear and limiting title, and each step begins with an action verb. The writer describes what happens on the screen and then gives users an example.

Sections 11.1.1–11.1.2 explain the format of a description block, the rules to follow in setting one up, and guidelines for specifying description blocks in a description file.

Section 11.1.2 discusses the **MAKE** description files that the QuickC environment builds for programs created within the environment.

11.1.1   Building a MAKE Description File

To illustrate how the **MAKE** utility works, this section describes how to build a simple **MAKE** description file. Since a **MAKE** description file is a text file, you can use any text editor to create one.

In this example, assume that you want to update an executable file named UPDATE.EXE whenever any of its source files are changed. Assume further that the names of these source files are GETINPUT.C, FINDREC.C, and UPDATE.C. Use the following procedure to create a **MAKE** description file to update UPDATE.EXE automatically:

1. Using the text editor, create a file named UPDATE. Although a **MAKE** description file can have any name, you may find it helpful to give the description file the same name (without an extension) as the file it maintains.

2. Type the name of the file you are maintaining followed by a colon, as shown below. This file is known as the "outfile," since **MAKE** creates the updated version of the file as output. (Outfiles are sometimes known as "target files.")

    UPDATE.EXE :

3. Following the colon, type the names of any files that, when changed, should cause the outfile to be updated. In this example, you want to update UPDATE.EXE whenever GETINPUT.C, FINDREC.C, or UPDATE.C is changed, so the line in the description file would look like this:

    UPDATE.EXE : UPDATE.C GETINPUT.C FINDREC.C

    The files to the right of the colon are known as "infiles" since **MAKE** uses them as input to determine whether or not to update the outfile. (Infiles are sometimes known as "dependent files.") Each infile is separated from the next by a space.

4. Type a number sign (#) if you want to add a comment to any line in a **MAKE** description file. **MAKE** ignores any text between the

Figure 19.3. Procedure with Examples (from *Microsoft QuickC Programmer's Guide*). The procedure has a specific title. Although modifying phrases begin some of the steps, each step is a direct command. The writer uses an extended example throughout the procedure.

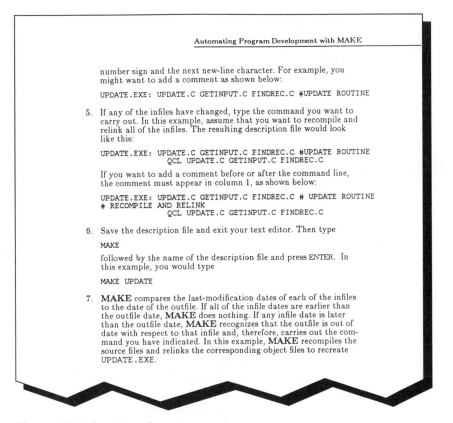

Figure 19.3 (continued).

Figure 19.3 shows another procedure that includes an example. The final illustration, Figure 19.4, shows a lengthy procedure that includes an extended example with several illustrations. (You can see more examples of procedures in Chapter 10, "Organizing Tutorials," and Chapter 11, "Organizing Procedures Guides.")

Newsletters

This sub-section describes how to create newsletter chapters. A news-letter chapter contains multiple articles, each saved in a different text file. These articles can start on any page and can continue on any later page. Each portion of each article can be placed in a frame anywhere in the chapter. Each frame can have its own set of margin, column, and vertical rule settings.

Newsletter Layout

Newsletters, newspapers, and magazines combine a variety of different typographic styles, column widths, and margins. You can generate this type of complex layout by placing text into frames, rather than directly onto the page. For those familiar with the traditional publishing process, this strategy very closely mimics the process of pasting up galleys on a page: once you draw a frame and place text into it, the frame becomes a galley that can be "pasted" anywhere on the page.

To compose a newsletter layout:

1) Follow the first seven steps for the book strategy shown on page 6-8.

2) Use the **Margin & Column** option in the Frame menu to provide column guides to which frames can be *snapped* (Figure 6–6). Turn **Show Column Guides On** to show these guides on the screen. In the book approach, the column settings are used to format the text on the page. In this approach, the column settings provide a grid to align the separate frames which you will manually draw. You will then place the respective text files into these frames.

3) Use the **Add New Frame** command in the Side-bar to place frames wherever you want text to appear (Figure 6–7).

4) Place text or pictures into each frame that you drew in the last step (Figure 6–8). To place text in a frame, select a frame, then select a file name from the Assignment List.

6-10   REFERENCE GUIDE

Figure 19.4. Procedure with an Illustrated Example (from *Xerox Ventura Publisher Reference Guide*). In this lengthy procedure, notice the clear title, the action verbs that begin each step, and the use of an extended example with several illustrations clarifying some of the steps.

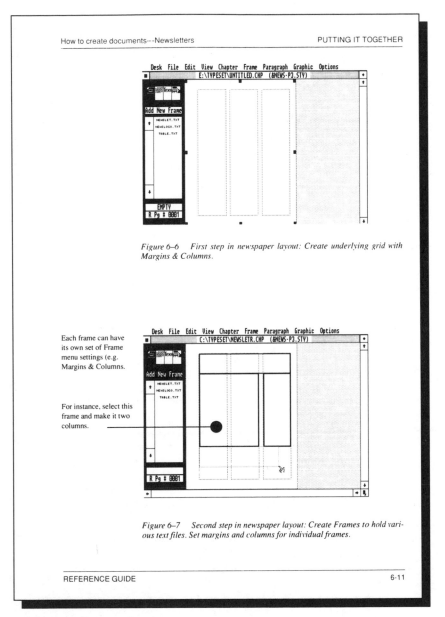

How to create documents--Newsletters   PUTTING IT TOGETHER

Desk File Edit View Chapter Frame Paragraph Graphic Options

E:\TYPESET\UNTITLED.CHP   (&NEWS-P3.STY)

Add New Frame

MEWSLET.TXT

MEWSLOGO.TXT

TABLE.TXT

EMPTY

R Pg # 0001

Figure 6–6   First step in newspaper layout: Create underlying grid with Margins & Columns.

Each frame can have its own set of Frame menu settings (e.g. Margins & Columns.

For instance, select this frame and make it two columns.

Desk File Edit View Chapter Frame Paragraph Graphic Options

C:\TYPESET\NEWSLETR.CHP   (&NEWS-P3.STY)

Add New Frame

MEWSLET.TXT

MEWSLOGO.TXT

TABLE.TXT

R Pg # 0001

Figure 6–7   Second step in newspaper layout: Create Frames to hold various text files. Set margins and columns for individual frames.

REFERENCE GUIDE   6-11

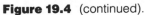

Figure 19.4 (continued).

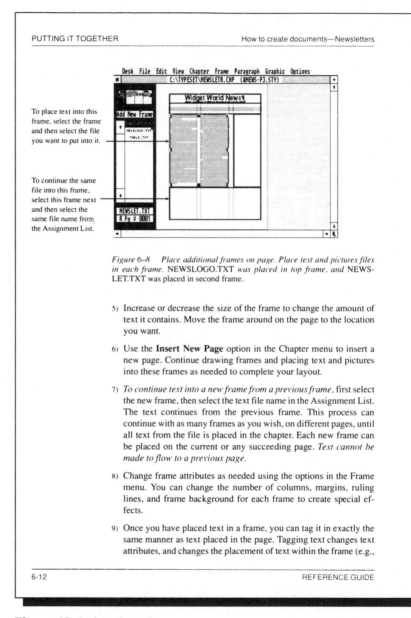

To place text into this frame, select the frame and then select the file you want to put into it.

To continue the same file into this frame, select this frame next and then select the same file name from the Assignment List.

Figure 6–8   Place additional frames on page. Place text and pictures files in each frame. NEWSLOGO.TXT *was placed in top frame, and* NEWS-LET.TXT *was placed in second frame.*

5) Increase or decrease the size of the frame to change the amount of text it contains. Move the frame around on the page to the location you want.

6) Use the **Insert New Page** option in the Chapter menu to insert a new page. Continue drawing frames and placing text and pictures into these frames as needed to complete your layout.

7) *To continue text into a new frame from a previous frame,* first select the new frame, then select the text file name in the Assignment List. The text continues from the previous frame. This process can continue with as many frames as you wish, on different pages, until all text from the file is placed in the chapter. Each new frame can be placed on the current or any succeeding page. *Text cannot be made to flow to a previous page.*

8) Change frame attributes as needed using the options in the Frame menu. You can change the number of columns, margins, ruling lines, and frame background for each frame to create special effects.

9) Once you have placed text in a frame, you can tag it in exactly the same manner as text placed in the page. Tagging text changes text attributes, and changes the placement of text within the frame (e.g.,

Figure 19.4 (continued).

How to create documents—Newsletters   PUTTING IT TOGETHER

right justified, centered.) All tag spacing is measured from the edge of the *frame*, not from the edge of the page. You can set the Page Break feature (Breaks option, Paragraph menu) to force text into the next frame.

If you want to annotate the information in a frame, switch to Graphic mode. *Select the frame* and then draw arrows, circles, box text, etc. to enhance the text or picture in the frame. Use the Text features to edit text in frames and text in box text.

Figures 6–6, 6–7, and 6–8 show how to compose part of the first page of a newsletter.

When placing te~·   ~ame file into ~·   ~s on the same

Figure 19.4 (continued).

PART FOUR

INFORMATION FORMS

FORM 1: PROJECT OVERVIEW

FORM 2: DOCUMENTATION PROJECT
PERSONNEL

FORM 3: DOCUMENTATION SCHEDULE

FORM 4: DOCUMENT DESCRIPTION

FORM 5: DOCUMENTATION SET
DESCRIPTION

FORM 6: AUDIENCE PROFILE

FORM 7: INTERFACE DESCRIPTION

FORM 8: PROGRAM FEATURES

FORM 9: PROBLEM SUPPORT SYSTEM

FORM 10: HELP SYSTEM DESCRIPTION

This section contains forms that you can photocopy and use for all your documentation projects. When you complete a set of forms for a project, you'll find that you have the information necessary for efficient planning.

PROJECT OVERVIEW

Project name _____

Brief description of project _____

_____

_____

Why was this project initiated? _____

_____

_____

_____

_____

_____

Brief description of user interface design _____

_____

_____

_____

_____

_____

Other comments about project _____

_____

_____

_____

_____

DOCUMENTATION PROJECT PERSONNEL

Document name _____

Manager(s) _____ Phone _____

_____ Phone _____

Programmer(s) _____ Phone _____

_____ Phone _____

Writer(s) _____ Phone _____

_____ Phone _____

Reviewers _____ Phone _____

_____ Phone _____

_____ Phone _____

_____ Phone _____

_____ Phone _____

Editor _____ Phone _____

Proofreader _____ Phone _____

Word processor(s) _____ Phone _____

_____ Phone _____

Artist _____ Phone _____

Production supervisor _____ Phone _____

Scheduler _____ Phone _____

Other(s) _____ Phone _____

_____ Phone _____

_____ Phone _____

_____ Phone _____

DOCUMENTATION SCHEDULE

Document name _____

First review date   _____   Note _____

_____   Note _____

_____   Note _____

Second review date _____   Note _____

_____   Note _____

_____   Note _____

Final review date _____

Editing/proofreading completed _____

All corrections made/hand-off to production staff _____

Books complete/ready for delivery _____

Notes _____

_____

_____

_____

_____

_____

_____

DOCUMENT DESCRIPTION

Complete a form for each printed piece of documentation.

Title of document _____

Estimated page length _____

Production Information:

How will pages of document be reproduced? _____
(photocopy, offset printing, other)

How will text be created? _____
(word processing program, text editor, other)

How will typeset pages be produced? _____
(laser printer, commercial typesetter, imageset)

How will pages be made up? _____
(desktop publishing, traditional paste-up, other)

What types of illustrations will be used? _____

_____
(line art, halftone art, photographs, screen shots, tables)

How will document be bound?

   Three-ring binder _____ Size _____

   Brad-type binder _____

   Spiral binding   _____ Size _____

   Perfect binding   _____ Soft or hard cover _____

   Other _____

Page Layout:

Attach document specifications and sample pages, if available.

Page size _____

Live-matter area (area containing any text) _____

Number of heading levels _____ Sideheads _____

Columns:

   Multiple-column tables _____

   Two-column procedures _____

   Two-column lists _____

Special typestyles (bold, italics, full caps, small caps, contrasting typestyle):

Element   Format

_____   _____

_____   _____

_____   _____

_____   _____

_____   _____

_____   _____

_____   _____

_____   _____

What types of illustrations can the writer use? _____
(diagrams, concept drawings, photographs, screen shots, tables, charts, graphs)

Maximum size of illustrations _____

Special graphic treatments (boxes, screen tints, second-color ink, lines and rules, other):

Element   Treatment

_____   _____

_____   _____

_____   _____

_____   _____

_____   _____

DOCUMENTATION SET DESCRIPTION

Project name _____

Printed documents

_____ No. of pages _____

_____ No. of pages _____

_____ No. of pages _____

_____ No. of pages _____

_____ No. of pages _____

_____ No. of pages _____

_____ No. of pages _____

On-line materials

_____ No. of screens _____

_____ No. of screens _____

_____ No. of screens _____

_____ No. of screens _____

Packaging notes

_____

_____

_____

_____

AUDIENCE PROFILE

Primary Group:

Job title(s) _____

_____

_____

Knowledge of computer hardware and software that these users probably already have

_____

_____

_____

Reasons these people might buy this product _____

_____

_____

_____

Features that would especially interest these people _____

_____

_____

_____

Secondary Group:

Job title(s) _____

_____

_____

Knowledge of computer hardware and software that these users probably already have

_____

_____

_____

Reasons these people might buy this product _____

_____

_____

Features that would especially interest these people _____

_____

_____

_____

INTERFACE DESCRIPTION

Photocopy and fill out as many forms as necessary.

Menu or screen name (if appropriate) _____

Command or field name _____

Description of how it works _____

_____

_____

Associated options, switches, or variables _____

_____

_____

_____

_____

_____

Conditions that affect the command or field _____

_____

_____

Shortcuts or other ways to use _____

_____

_____

PROGRAM FEATURES

List major features of the program on this form.

Feature _____

Why is this a key feature? _____

_____

Feature _____

Why is this a key feature? _____

_____

Feature _____

Why is this a key feature? _____

_____

Feature _____

Why is this a key feature? _____

_____

Feature _____

Why is this a key feature? _____

_____

Feature _____

Why is this a key feature? _____

_____

Feature _____

Why is this a key feature? _____

_____

Feature _____

Why is this a key feature? _____

_____

Feature _____

Why is this a key feature? _____

_____

Feature _____

Why is this a key feature? _____

_____

Feature _____

Why is this a key feature? _____

_____

Feature _____

Why is this a key feature? _____

_____

PROBLEM SUPPORT SYSTEM

What do users do to cancel a command or choice? _____

_____

_____

What should users do if the system crashes? _____

_____

_____

How can users find out what a screen message means? _____

_____

_____

How can users cancel printing and other processes? _____

_____

_____

Notes about other potential problems that users may encounter _____

_____

_____

What phone number can users call to get help? _____

HELP SYSTEM DESCRIPTION

Project name _____

Who is responsible for help system text? _____

_____

_____

Who is responsible for help system implementation and testing? _____

_____

_____

How will users access the help system? _____

_____

_____

_____

How will users display different screens of help information? _____

_____

_____

How will users know where they are in the help system? _____

_____

_____

How will users exit from the help system? _____

_____

_____

Help system screen design notes _____

_____

_____

_____

Other features of help system (searching, printing, bookmarking, ability to add or delete
text, and so forth) _____

_____

_____

_____

Other comments about help system _____

_____

_____

_____

RESOURCES

BOOKS

Dictionaries

Shaw, Harry. *Dictionary of Problem Words and Expressions.* Rev. ed. New York: McGraw-Hill, 1987.

Webster's Ninth New Collegiate Dictionary. 9th ed. Springfield, Mass.: Merriam-Webster, 1985. A standard abridged dictionary.

Webster's Third New International Dictionary, Unabridged: The Great Library of the English Language. Springfield, Mass.: Merriam-Webster, 1986. A standard unabridged dictionary.

Style Manuals

The Chicago Manual of Style. 13th ed. Chicago: University of Chicago Press, 1982.

Jordan, Lewis. *The New York Times Manual of Style and Usage.* New York: Times Books, 1982.

Skillin, M., and R. Gay. *Words into Type.* 3rd ed. Englewood Cliffs, N.J.: Prentice-Hall, 1974.

Writing and Editing

Beason, Pamela S., and Patricia A. Williams. *Technical Writing for Business and Industry.* Chicago: Scott, Foresman, 1989.

Cook, Claire Kehrwald. *Line by Line: The MLA's Guide to Improving Your Writing.* Boston: Houghton Mifflin, 1985.

Ebbett, Wilma R., and David R. Ebbett. *Writer's Guide and Index to English.* 7th ed. Chicago: Scott, Foresman, 1982.

Strunk, William, Jr., and E. B. White. *The Elements of Style.* 3rd ed. New York: Macmillan, 1979.

Graphics and Print Production

Beach, Mark, Steve Shepro, and Ken Russon. *Getting It Printed: How to Work with Printers and Graphic Art Services to Assure Quality, Stay on Schedule, and Control Costs*. Portland, Ore.: Coast to Coast Books, 1986.

Campbell, Alastair. *The Graphic Designer's Handbook*. New rev. ed. Philadelphia: Running Press, 1988.

Lem, Dean Phillip. *Graphics Master*. 4th ed. Los Angeles: Dean Lem Associates, 1988.

Sanders, Norman. *Graphic Designer's Production Handbook*. New York: Hasting House Publishers, 1983.

White, Jan V. *Mastering Graphics*. New York: R. R. Bowker, 1983.

Desktop Publishing

Kleper, Michael L. *The Illustrated Handbook of Desktop Publishing and Typesetting*. Blue Ridge Summit, Penn.: TAB Professional and Reference Books, 1987.

Lang, Kathy. *The Writer's Guide to Desktop Publishing*. Orlando, Fla.: Academic Press, 1987.

PERIODICALS

Writing and Editing

Technical Communications Journal: Society for Technical Communications, Williams & Wilkins Company, 428 E. Preston Street, Baltimore, MD 21202

Design and Production

The Desktop: 342 East Third Street, Loveland, CO 80537

Desktop Publishing & Office Automation: Buyer's Guide and Handbook: Computer Information Publishing Inc., 150 Fifth Avenue, New York, NY 10011

In-House Graphics: 342 East Third Street, Loveland, CO 80537

Personal Publishing: Hitchcock Publishing Company, 25W550 Geneva Road, Wheaton, IL 60188

Publish!: PCW Communications, Inc., 501 Second St., San Francisco, CA 94107

GLOSSARY

action verb A verb in the active voice, where the subject of the sentence performs the action

anaphora A writing device where the beginning phrases of two or more sentences are identical; a type of *parallelism*

blueline In printing, a copy of a document produced before the final print run so you can check print quality

bookmarking A feature provided by some software that lets you mark a location in a file so you can easily "jump" to or reference that marked location

callout Text that describes or explains one of the elements in an illustration; usually linked to the element by a line, arrow, or reference mark

caption The title that appears directly above or below an illustration; can also refer to all the information that identifies or explains the illustration

conventions In software documentation, the set of formats used for characters (variables, for instance) and terms (commands, for instance) so readers can instantly recognize each category

galleys In typesetting, a copy of the text, usually not spaced or paginated in its final form, that lets you see if the text has been properly typeset

gutter margin A margin on the inside of each page large enough to accommodate the binding; located on the left on a right-hand page, on the right on a left-hand page

icon In software, a small graphic symbol used in place of text (an icon of a disk might represent a disk drive, for instance)

interface The format used to present software to users on the computer screen together with the method used to control the software

justification On the printed page, when both left and right margins are aligned

keyboard template A printed cutout that fits around a keyboard, listing important keys or commands

leading In printed materials, the space between lines of type

legend In a *caption*, the text that explains the illustration

noun cluster Several nouns grouped together where a single noun would do, producing a pretentious tone

parallelism A writing device that shows the relationship of ideas by repeating grammatical structure either within a sentence, a paragraph, or two or more separate paragraphs

passive verb   A verb in the passive voice, where the subject of the sentence is acted upon; used chiefly when the performer of the action is unknown or unimportant

perfect binding   A method of binding a document where the pages are bound together and affixed to the cover by adhesive

pica   A typographical unit of measurement that is $\frac{1}{16}$ of an inch; six picas roughly equal 1 inch (0.996")

point   The smallest ($\frac{1}{72}$ inch) typographical unit of measurement; twelve points equal 1 *pica*

prepositional phrase   A phrase beginning with a preposition, such as *of, as, in*

primary readers   The most important readers of a document, sometimes the majority, sometimes those who make the most use of the document

procedures guide   A type of document or a section in a document that explains and gives step-by-step instructions on how to perform all the functions of the program

profile   A description of the readers or the audience for a document

quick reference   A card, keyboard template, or booklet that lists the most frequently used commands, functions, or key assignments

ragged right   On the printed page, when the right margin is unaligned

README file   In software, a file named **README** containing information about any software developments that may have occurred after the documentation was printed

redundancy   In writing, the unnecessary repetition of words or phrases that have the same meaning

reference   A type of document or a section in a document that describes in detail commands, functions, fields, options, key assignments, and/or messages

reverse type   In printing, light-colored text against a dark background

rule   In typography, a line used for an effect, including the creation of borders and boxes; measured in *points* of thickness

running foot   Text that appears at the bottom of every page; can include information such as a page number, a document title, or a chapter head

running head   Text that appears at the top of every page; can include information such as a page number, document title, or chapter head

sans serif   A typeface in which the characters do not have *serifs*

scenario   In a *tutorial*, the "plot" or projected sequence of events

screen shot   A printout of everything that appears on a particular computer screen, used as an illustration; sometimes called a screen capture or a screen dump

screen tint   In printing, a shaded area created by breaking up color into dots so that ink coverage is less than 100 percent

serifs   The curves and flourishes on characters in some typefaces

specifications   A description of the design of a document that specifies measurements, type, and materials; used as a guide for print production

style guide   A compendium of guidelines on spelling, punctuation, and usage; used to ensure consistency and accuracy in the writing, editing, and proofreading of a document

transitions   Words and phrases that express relationships between one idea and another

trim size   The final size of the printed page

tutorial   A type of document or a section in a document that teaches basic program functions through controlled "hands-on" practice sessions

typeface   A set of characters with design features that make them similar to one another

white space   Blank space on the printed page that is an integral part of the design

INDEX